THE EVOLUTION OF PARLIAMENT IN GHANA

THE EVOLUTION OF PARLIAMENT IN GHANA

K. B. Ayensu and S. N. Darkwa

Sub-Saharan Publishers

First published in Ghana in 1999 by
The Institute of Economic Affairs (IEA)

This revised edition published in 2006 by
Sub-Saharan Publishers
P. O. Box LG 358
Legon, Accra

© Copyright text: K.B. Ayensu, S.N. Darkwa 1999

ISBN 9988- 550-76-6

All rights reserved. No part of this publication may be reproduced, stored in a retrieval system or transmitted in any form or by any means electronic, mechanical, photocopying, recording or otherwise, without the prior permission of the publishers.

Layout and cover design: Kwabena Agyepong

Printed in Mauritius by Book Printing Services Ltd

CONTENTS

Preface	009
The New Edition	010
Biographical Notes on the Authors (by Justice P. D. Anin)	011

Part One: Genesis of the First Parliament of Ghana and The Story of the Six Others — 013

1. The Bond of 1844 — 015
2. Seven Parliaments, Could Have Been Nine — 016
3. Exercise of Legislative Power in Ghana — 016
4. The Trek to Nationhood — 018
5. The Building of a Launching pad — 022
6. Danquah and Nkrumah: Divergent Visions of the Same Goal — 022
7. Grant, Danquah and Nkrumah – Their Memorials — 023
8. Tragedy of the Crossroads — 024
9. The Tragedy Compounded by Boycott — 025
10. Detention of the "Big Six" — 025
11. Commission of Enquiry and Constitutional Committee — 025
12. An Honourable Member at 25 — 027
13. Antenatal Problems — 027
14. The Name of the Child and the Date of Birth — 028
15. Dispersal of the Post – 1954 General Election Clouds — 029
16. The Ghana Independence Act, 1957 — 030
17. The Ghana (Constitution) Order in Council, 1957 — 030
18. Confrontation: Governor Versus Clerk of Parliament — 031
19. Arrival of the Queen's Special Representative — 031
20. Rehearsal for the Duchess of Kent — 032
21. The Day Before THE DAY — 032
22. The Independence Vigil — 033
23. The Independence Parliament: March 6, 1957 — 034
24. State Opening of the Independence Parliament: March 6, 1957 — 035
25. A Memorable Occasion for Speaker Quist Opening of the New House of Commons — 037
26. Resignation and Death of Speaker Quist — 038
27. Election of New Speaker — 038
28. Resignation of Deputy Speaker Chapman — 039
29. Preparation for the Establishment of Regional Assemblies — 039
30. The Inter-Parliamentary Union — 039
31. The Commonwealth Parliamentary Association — 040
32. The Preventive Detention Act, 1958 — 040

33.	Presentation of a Speaker's Chair to Parliament	041
34.	Aftermath of the Deportation Orders of October 20, 1958	041
35.	The Constituent Assembly and Plebiscite Act, 1960	041
36.	Kwame Nkrumah and the Importance of Legal Cover	041
37.	Nkrumah Presses on the Goal	043
38.	Lessons From the Past	044
39.	The First Women Members of Parliament	045
40.	Resignation of Speaker Akiwumi	046
41.	Parliament and the "African Personality"	047
42.	The Day Before REPUBLIC DAY	047
43.	The First Parliament of the First Republic: July 2 1960	050
44.	First Sitting of the First Parliament of the First Republic	051
45.	State Opening of the First Parliament of the First Republic: July 5, 1960	052
46.	Last Sitting of the First Parliament of the First Republic	052
47.	Highlights of the First Parliament of the First Republic	054
48.	The Second Parliament of the First Republic; August 24, 1965	054
49.	The First Sitting of the Second Parliament of the First Republic	056
50.	State Opening of the Second Parliament of the First Republic; August 24, 1965	057
51.	Attendance of the Speaker at the 700th Anniversary Celebrations in London	057
52.	Last Sitting of the Second Parliament of the First Republic	058
53.	Highlights of the Second Parliament of the First Republic	059
54.	Preparation for a Return to Parliament	059
55.	The First Parliament of the Second Republic: October 2, 1969	060
56.	First Sitting of the Parliament of the Second Republic	062
57.	State Opening of the First Parliament of the Second Republic: October 2, 1969	062
58.	Highlights of the Parliament of the Second Republic	064
59.	A Second Preparation for a Return to Parliament	065
60.	The First Parliament of the Third Republic: September 24, 1979	065
61.	First Sitting of the Parliament of the Third Republic: and Inauguration of the Third Republic:	

	September 24, 1979	067
62.	Highlights of the Parliament of the Third Republic	070
63.	A Third Preparation for a Return to Parliament	071
64.	The First Parliament of the Fourth Republic: January 7, 1993	072
65.	First Sitting of the First Parliament of the Fourth Republic	075
66.	State Opening of the First Parliament of the Fourth Republic: April 29, 1993	075
67.	Some Highlights of the First Parliament of the Fourth Republic	077
68.	The 1996 General Elections	081
69.	First Sitting of the Second Parliament of the Fourth Republic	084
70.	State Opening of the Second Parliament of the Fourth Republic: January 21, 1997	086
71.	Highlights of the Second Parliament of the Fourth Republic	088
72.	Reflections on Opposition Boycott	092
73.	The Third Parliament of the Fourth Republic. The 2000 Elections – Consolidation of Multi-Party	093
74.	The First Sitting of Third Parliament of the Fourth Republic	097
75.	The First Message to Parliament on the State of the Nation, February 15, 2001	099
76.	Parliament and the media	101
77.	Some Highlights of the Third Parliament of the Fourth Republic	102
78.	Parliament, The Speaker and the Clerk	103
79.	From the Clerk's Diary: Parliamentary English	108
80.	Ghana is Forty Years, but What Does the Future Hold?	108

Part Two: Development of the Parliamentary system in Ghana under the Four Republics — **111**

81.	The 1957 Independence Constitution	112
82.	The 1960 Republican Constitution	112
83.	Castigation of Parliament Under the First Republic	113
84.	The 1969 Constitution	114
85.	The 1979 Constitution	116
86.	The 1992 Constitution	117
87.	Some Comparisons Between the Four Republics	118
88.	The Committee System	119
89.	The Development of Committees	119
90.	Committees of Parliament of the First Republic	120

91.	House Committee, Committee of Privileges, Public Accounts Committee, Business Committee, Standing Orders Committee	120
92.	The Committee System after the First Republic	121
93.	Committees of Parliament of the Fourth Republic	122
94.	Comparisons between Standing Committees of the House of Commons and the Ghana Parliament	122
95.	Membership of Committees Reflects Party Strengths in the House	123
96.	Chairmen of Committees	123
97.	Size of Committees	123
98.	Non-Partisan Approach to Work in the Public Accounts Committee	124
99.	Select Committees	124
100.	Meetings of Committees	124
101.	Committee of Whole House	124
102.	General Powers of Select Committees	125
103.	Advantages of the Committee System	126
104.	A Hybrid of Westminster and Congress System of Government in Ghana	128

Appendices   **135**

105.	Tribute to the late K. B. Ayensu (by S.N. Darkwa)	136
106.	Parliament stands undissolved while Ghana goes to the polls (by S.N. Darkwa)	137
107.	The Constitution, and not Parliament, is supreme (by S.N. Darkwa)	141

PREFACE

The Evolution of Parliament in Ghana contains two papers contributed jointly by parliamentary technocrats, S.N. Darkwa, Clerk of Parliament, and K.B. Ayensu, some time Clerk of Parliament. The material in this book is neither easily obtainable nor generally available. Some of it derives from experience gained on the job, personal exposure to situations, and private papers. Putting all the material together in one book is of great advantage.

Legislative power was exercised in the Gold Coast in colonial circumstances between 1850 and 1957. Its cessation occurred in a dramatic manner with the prorogation of Parliament at a quarter before midnight on the eve of Independence Day (March 6, 1957). Out went a colonial legislature and in came a sovereign one.

The formation of the United Gold Coast Convention (UGCC) in 1947 and the Convention People's Party (CPP) in 1949 heightened the struggle for independence, gave it a new dimension, and activated the people including the grassroots ones. The 1951 Parliament (Legislative Assembly), which was established after the first meaningful general election held that year, jolted the masses into an awareness of existence of an institution of measureless might and majesty.

The parliamentary system of government was curtailed in 1966 when the CPP Government was overthrown by the Armed Forces. The two parliaments which existed between 1966 and 1993 had a total life of four years and five months. The 1993 Parliament lived out its statutory life of four years, and the Second Parliament under the same Republic started business on January 7, 1997. The popular interest in Parliament which, like an unpredictable tide, flowed and ebbed irregularly between 1951 and 1993, has happily revived and is growing apace.

The decisions of Parliament affect the lives of all of us, and to understand that institution properly, one should know its history. That places this book in the pigeonhole of the recommended reading. It will doubtless be helpful to fiery politicians and sedate concerned citizens; public officers and people in various vocations; tutors and students; city-dwellers and rural folk; teenagers and octogenarians; any gender limitation being always especially and essentially excepted.

It is legitimate to state that the possession of decent knowledge of Parliament is nine-tenths of the prestige associated with membership.

THE NEW EDITION

The new edition has been updated to include the inauguration of the Third parliament of the Fourth Republic, which also saw the inauguration of President J.A. Kufuor. We felt that the elections of 2000, the third in succession, were significant. They marked a steady progress towards the consolidation of our multiparty democratic governance since the adoption of 1992 Constitution of the Fourth Republic. The smooth transfer of political power from a democratically elected government to another has eluded Ghana since Independence in 1957. For the first time in our history Ghana was able to hold three successive multiparty elections and the first peaceful change of government.

There is also an article on Ghana's hybrid system of government indicating some of its strengths and weaknesses. We have provided pictures of our Presidents and Speakers who have shaped the destiny of our country for the benefit of readers particularly the young generation and posterity.

We wish to acknowledge with gratitude the invaluable suggestions made by Dr. Baffour Agyemang-Duah, Associate Director of the Centre for Democratic Development (CDD). A former close colleague, Mr. S.O. Dodoo, for many years Editor of Parliamentary Debates (Hansard), and Mr. McJewels Annan, a Senior Officer of Parliament who diligently read the work in proof. We are indebted to Mr. D.A. Kwapong, Director of the Information Department and Mr. Stanley Felton, Managing Director of the African Market who provided the pictures of the Presidents and Speakers for the book. My former Secretary, Ms. Liz Andzie-Quainoo carefully typed the new edition.

Finally, we wish to thank Mr. K.E.K. Tachie, the Clerk to Parliament and his colleagues for their unstinted support and encouragement to bring the new edition into fruition.

Accra, 2004

BIOGRAPHICAL NOTES ON THE AUTHORS
by Justice P.D. Anin

K.B. Ayensu

The late K.B. Ayensu (known affectionately to his many friends, Masonic brothers, parliamentarians of the past half century, diplomats, statesmen and bureaucrats simply as "K.B.") was born on January 17, 1921 at Anomabo, the birthplace of the illustrious Dr. Kwegyir-Aggrey of blessed memory. He was educated at Adisadel College, Cape Coast and at Hertford College, Oxford University from whose Honour School of Jurisprudence he graduated Bachelor of Arts in 1946.

After a brief stint in the Gold Coast Public Service, he joined the Colonial Parliamentary Service as Deputy Clerk of Parliament in 1953. After only two years' efficient devoted service as Deputy Clerk, he was promoted to the exalted office of the Clerk of Parliament in 1955, a position he held till the overthrow of the Government in 1966. Thus it fell to his lot to ring out the Parliamentary Service of colonial Gold Coast and to ring in the new one of sovereign Ghana on March 6, 1957. "K.B" continued to serve as the first and only Clerk of Parliament throughout the regime of Dr. Kwame Nkrumah. With the latter's overthrow in Ghana's first coup d'etat on February 24, 1966 the incoming N.L.C. Administration retained "K.B's" service even though Parliament was dissolved by decree at the start of the revolution. From then until his retirement from the Public Service, "K.B." carved a niche for himself as the Chief of State Protocol with the rank of ambassador.

As a resource person in parliamentary practice since 1954, he gained experience in this field in many parts of the world; travelled widely on parliamentary delegations; and participated actively in seminars for MPs, the Parliamentary Press Corps, etc. Upon his retirement he devoted more time and energy to the task he probably enjoyed most: lecturing on parliamentary practice. Eventually, he acquired a huge reputation as the local "Erskine May" on parliamentary practice.

Readers of this book are indeed lucky that he found time and energy to contribute to this work; especially while a widower in his last year (1997) on earth. May he rest in perfect peace.

Samuel Ntim Darkwa

Samuel Ntim Darkwa was born on July 20, 1935 at Abofour in the Offinso District of Ashanti Region, and received his secondary education at Adisadel College, like his mentor and predecessor in office (Ayensu). Thereafter he graduated B.A. in Philosophy in 1961 at the University of Ghana, Legon.

He was thereupon recruited into the Ghana Parliamentary Service as Assistant Clerk in 1961. Having served Ayensu as Assistant Clerk from 1961 to 1966, he was promoted Deputy Clerk of Parliament in 1979, and Clerk in 1993. While parliament was in suspension after the overthrow of the 2nd Republic, Darkwa was seconded to the Commonwealth Secretariat, from 1975 to 1978. He was Assistant Clerk to the 1968 Constituent Assembly, Deputy Clerk to 1978 Constituent Assembly, and Clerk to the 1992 Consultative Assembly. He thus holds the unique record of having served all the Parliaments and Constituent Assemblies between 1961 and 1997.

Darkwa attracted considerable attention by his highly-rated January 1997 article on the recent problems created by the Fourth Republican Parliament's continued existence after its mandatory four-year life had expired at the date of the recent general elections by virtue of Article 113 (1) and (3) of the Fourth Republican Constitution. The late Ayensu made a valuable suggestion and recommendation for possible amendment.

He has participated in several conferences of the Commonwealth Parliamentary Workshop/Seminar in Southern Africa wherein he was a resource person. He is also a regular contributor to "The Parliamentarian," the leading journal for Commonwealth Parliamentarians.

Darkwa's expertise in parliamentary practice and procedures, especially in the inner workings of the whole House and its Committees, has been acknowledged by his peers, not only in Ghana but indeed throughout the British Commonwealth.

He was a great friend and loyal disciple of the late Ayensu, his erstwhile mentor and guide. That friendship lasted till the demise of the latter. Ayensu and Darkwa also share authorship of the book: "How our Parliament Fuctions".

PART ONE:

GENESIS OF THE FIRST PARLIAMENT OF GHANA AND THE STORY OF THE SIX OTHERS

Sir Emmanuel Quist
First Speaker of Parliament of Ghana

THE MACE OF PARLIAMENT OF GHANA

Symbol of Authority of Parliament. The design of the Ghana mace is made up of various Ghanaian traditional symbols.

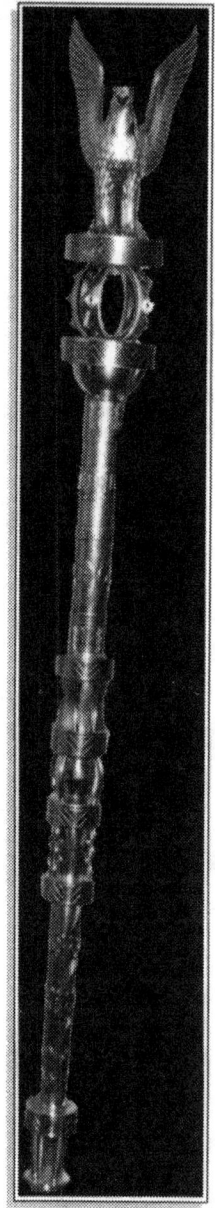

The Flying Eagle, symbolising the State of Ghana.
"Kontonkurowi" symbol of the common sharing of responsibility.
"Nyamedua", symbol of critical examination.
"Gye-Nyame", (except God), a symbol of the omnipotence of God.
"Kudu-Pono", a symbol of lasting personality.
"Mbaadwa" a symbol of the presence and effect of feminine power in society
"Dwanimmen", a symbol of manly strength.
"Hye-Wo-Nhye", (burnt but unburnt), symbol of imperishability .
"Bi-Nka-Bi", (no one bites another), symbol of justice.
"Kuntun-Kantan", (bent only to straighten), symbol of the pride of State.

There are no acts of treachery more deeply concealed than those which lie under the pretence of duty, or under some profession of necessity.

Cicero

THE BOND OF 1844
The Basis of British Jurisdiction in the Gold Coast
BOND, 6TH MARCH, 1844

1. "WHEREAS power and jurisdiction have been exercised for and on behalf of Her Majesty the Queen of Great Britain and Ireland, within diverse countries and places adjacent to Her Majesty's forts and settlements on the Gold Coast; we, Chiefs of countries and places so referred to, adjacent to such forts and settlements, do hereby acknowledge that power and jurisdiction and declare that the first objects of law are protection of individuals and property.
2. "Human sacrifices, and other barbarous customs, such as panyarring, are abominations contrary to law.
3. "Murders, robberies and other crimes and offences, will be tried and enquired before the Queen's judicial officers and the Chiefs of the districts, moulding the customs of the country to the general principles of British law.
4. "Done at Cape Coast Castle before His Excellency the Lieutenant-Governor, on this 6th day of March, in the year of our Lord 1844.

Their marks:
- Cudjoe Chibboe, King of Denkera
- Quashie Ottoo, Chief of Abura
- Chibboe Coomah, Chief of Assin
- Gebre, Second Chief of Assin
- Quashie Ankah, Chief of Donadie
- Awoosie, Chief of Dominassie
(Signed) Quarshie Ankah

Their marks:
- Amonoo, Chief of Anomabu
- Joe Aggrey, Chief of Cape Coast

"Witness my seal on the 6th day of March 1844, and the 7th year of Her Majesty's reign.
"(Signed) H.W. Hill, Lieutenant-Governor (L.S)
"And done in the presence of:
Witnesses
"(Signed) George Maclean, J.P. and Assessor (S)
"F. Pogoson, Lieut., 1st W.I. Regiment (S)
Commanding H.M. Troops
"S. Bannerman, Adjutant of Militia (S)."

Seven Parliaments, Could Have Been Nine

The Independence Parliament of 1957 was short-lived because of the people's anxiety to become a republic. That status was attained on July 1, 1960. If the Constitution on which the Republic was based had never been disturbed, the people would in 1997 be listening to debates in the eighth parliament of the Republic, and one would be telling the story of the nine parliaments of Ghana (that is to say truncated Independence parliament and eight five-year Parliaments under one Republic).

And yet, despite the considerable total of the periods of military rule, there have been as many as seven parliaments, namely the Independence Parliament (Nkrumah), the two Parliaments of the First republic (Nkrumah), the one Parliament of the Second Republic (Busia), the one Parliament of the Third Republic (Limann) and the two Parliaments of the Fourth Republic (Rawlings)

Exercise of Legislative Power in Ghana

A brief look into the 19th century in order to trace the history of legislative power in Ghana will be useful. Legislative power was first exercised in the Gold Coast during the reign of Queen Victoria (1837-9001). During the period 1850-1865 the Gold Coast, being for the first time a distinct dependency of the British Crown, had its own Legislative Council. It consisted of Governor and at least two other persons designated by Royal Instructions. It was required to make "all such laws, institutions and ordinances as may from time to time be necessary for the peace, order and good government of our subjects and others within the said present or future forts and settlements in the Gold Coast", subject to rules and regulations made by Order in

Council and to the right of the Crown to disallow any such ordinances, either in whole or in part, and with a saving for the future exercise of legislative power by an Act of Parliament or Order in Council.

Ordinances were to be styled: "ordinances enacted by the Governor of our Forts and Settlements on the Gold Coast, with Advice and Consent of the Legislative Council thereof". The Governor was required to withhold assent to any ordinance which was repugnant to any Act of British Parliament or to the Royal Charter or Royal Instructions, or which interfered with Christian worship, diminished public divorce, etc. With few exceptions no ordinance was to come into effect until the pleasure of the Crown had been signified. In 1850 the Gold Coast became a separate dependency of the British Crown. Its Governor was responsible to London. In that year it established a Legislative Council. The African unofficial members nominated to serve on it in the 19th century were:

James Bannerman, Merchant and Civil Commandant of Accra,
Lieutenant-Governor (December 1850 to September 1851) ... 1850 – 1856,
George Kuntu-Blankson, Merchant of Cape Coast ... 1861 – 1873,
Robert Hutcheson, merchant of Cape Coast ... 1861 – 1863,
Francis Chapman Grant, Merchant of Cape Coast... 1863 – 1866, 1871 – 1873, 1887 (as Extraordinary Member),
Samuel Collins Brew, Merchant of Anomabu ... 1864 – 1866,
George Cleland, Merchant of Accra and Divisional Chief of James Town ... 1886 – 1887,
William Hutchison, Merchant of Cape Coast... 1887 (as Extraordinary Member),
John Sarbah, Merchant of Anomabu and Cape Coast, 1887 (as Extraordinary Member) ... 1888 – 1892,
James Henry Cheetham, Merchant of Cape Coast, trading in Accra ... 1893 – 1898,
Chief John Vanderpuiye, Merchant of Accra and Divisional Chief of Ussher Town ... 1894 – 1904, and
Thomas Hutton-Mills, Barrister of Accra ... 1898 – 1900.

From 1866 to 1874 the Gold Coast was reunited with the West African Settlements and its Legislative Council was reduced in size. In 1874 the Gold Coast was again given a separate government. It was from then that the steady growth of the legislature began, but even quite near the end of the 19th century, the powers of the legislature were still limited and its area of authority undefined.

Under the 1946 Constitution, provision was made for an elected legislature, and Ashanti was for the first time given representation. In 1949 the Legislative Council was given jurisdiction over Southern Togoland under United Kingdom trusteeship. In 1951 the Legislative Council became the legislature of the northern Territories also. Before these changes, legislative jurisdiction over these areas resided exclusively in the Governor.

The Trek to Nationhood

To discover how the First Parliament of Ghana came about, one may ask: When did the trek begin? A hundred years before independence, the people started to move towards nationhood, even if feebly. They were going to counter the effects of the Bond of 1844 which marked the beginning of a march in the opposite direction. It took Israel 40 years to restore what she had lost. Ghanaians should consider themselves blessed that it took them ten years to regain their loss, doing a trek of different nature. In a sense 1844 – 1957 was like John Milton's Paradise Lost and Paradise Regained, with Samson Agonistes in between. Ghana had a fundamental problem with British unwillingness to free her colonies. When R. L. Stevenson wrote, "Independent America is still the cross of my existence, and I cannot think of Farmer George without the abhorrence," he meant he still got the needle when he thought that it was during the reign of George III that Britain lost its American colonies. Winston Churchill in his time felt the same as R.L.S. did about losing colonies.

The activities of the Fante Confederacy of 1868, the Fante Fekuw (Society) of 1885, the Aborigines' Rights Protection Society of 1897 and the Congress of British of West Africa of 1920, succeeded in promoting a consciousness of the national heritage. Their sphere of influence was small and they were up against many of our forebears who either scoffed at their endeavours or were happy with the British and in no particular hurry for self-rule.

All praise to the elders who, equipped only with fortitude and resolve, fought for self-rule, even if on a parochial basis. Take the case of King John Aggrey of Cape Coast who enjoyed the style and title of King Aggery of Cape Coast and its Dependencies. He was born in Cape Coast in 1809 to King Joseph Aggrey of Cape Coast, one of the chiefs who subscribed the Bond of 1844. He did not succeed his father directly but was installed King of Cape Coast in 1865. He was neither wealthy nor lettered but terribly outspoken and committed. In spite of the Bond, he made it clear to the British that they were trespassing on his land.

Cape Coast was then the capital of the Gold Coast. Aggrey ran his traditional administration and his court alongside similar British institutions. The Governor moved against Aggrey's court. Aggrey sought the support of other chiefs. The dedicated rebel was let down by them. They actually said: "To leave us now would be like the parent forsaking his offspring before being able to care for itself". The only king who stood by Aggrey was Otabil of Gomoa who suffered imprisonment in consequence.

Aggrey was not dismayed. He sent a deputation of two men to London and they appeared before a House of Commons Select Committee. But matters remained unsettled. In a defiant mood Aggrey wrote to the Governor Coran:

> "The time has now come for me to record a solemn protest against the perpetual annoyances and insults that you persistently continue to practise on me in my capacity as legally constituted King of Cape Coast.
>
> I presume your object is to incite me and my people to enact more of those fearful things that took place in Jamaica that I have heard of... However you may wish to have me and my people under martial laws, you will never have that pleasure...
>
> The Earl of Carnarvon has laid it down in his speech on the 2nd August last (1865) that we are all entitled to redress at his hands as the Colonial Minister. To that quarter I shall appeal for the last time, and then if some tangible satisfaction is not accorded to me and those interest I am bound to

protect, it will be time enough for me to adopt those measures which time enough for me to adopt those measures which will ensure to me and my people something unlike the slavery that your are endeavouring to place us in."

Strong words, but Aggrey did not stop at them. He sent a deputation of two men to the 1865 Select Committee of the House of Commons on Free Trade. He told the British Government in Cape Coast he intended to form his own military corps, to be trained by British officers, for his self-defence. London thought the Kong's language was seditious and ordered the Governor to put down this "insolent, ignorant and stubborn man." Aggrey continued to give the British much trouble. When they were saturated with his harassment, they removed him to Sierra Leone, a move about which London had misgivings. He returned to Cape Coast after two years and abdicated his reign. He died in the year of his return, 1869.

This is an epic about the 19th Century struggle for black emancipation. The hero bore the whip and scorn of British imperialists in an endeavour to get rid of them. Neither J.B. Danquah nor Kwame Nkrumah nor Bafour Osei Akoto would have affronted a governor with the vehemence of Chief John Aggrey of Cape Coast and its Dependencies. If he had been the King of Cape Coast in 1844, he certainly would not have subscribed the Bond.

A number of individuals who were highly motivated, including British-educated ones, worked hard towards self-assertion in certain spheres of national life. The Fante Society emphasized a revival of Fante cultural tradition in dress, language, music and people's names. A number of Fantes dropped their European names, urging that "educated Fantes" were preferable to "Europeanised natives". "Going Fante" or "having gone Fante" symbolised nationalism.

Patronizingly, the British gave their employees names they could pronounce. Kweku Dadzie (Steel) became Frank Steel. Ekow Hammah (Rope) became George Hammond. Kofi Kuntu (Blanket) became Frank Blankson. Some eventually resumed their original names or took hybrid ones, partly Fante and partly British. Thus George Hammond reverted to Ekow Hammah while Frank Steel became Steel Dadzie and Kofi Kuntu became

Kuntu Blankson. "Ayensu" being the name of a river (which is essentially water), a merchant called Kobina Ayensu had his name changed to John Waters. That was perhaps "the most unkindest cut of all". With the benefit of hindsight John Waters reverted to Kobina Ayensu and thus prevented the awkwardness of the First Clerk of the parliament of Ghana, a black native (popularly called "home-boy"), bearing the very British name, John Waters. A document recently researched by the authors, records that a British agent of the firm of F. and A. Swanzy (subsequently a constituent of United Africa Company), with which Kobina Ayensu worked, went by the name of William Waters. He lived long in the Colony, and was well known as a merchant prince and a Member of the Legislative Council. He did not think Ayensu would mind sharing his rather illustrious name. A number of newspapers, untrammelled by their own operational difficulties, made a significant contribution to the nationalist cause. The following are most of the newspapers that were involved in the crusade for self-determination.

> The Gold Coast Nation (afterwards The Gold Coast Times),
> The Gold Coast Methodist Times,
> The Gold Coast Chronicle,
> The Gold Coast Echo,
> The Gold Coast Observer,
> The Gold Coast Leader,
> The African Morning Post (afterwards The Gold Coast Spectator)
> The Spectator Daily
> Asenta,
> The Independence,
> Vox Populi,
> Star of West Africa,
> West African Herald, and
> Western Echo.

Two champions of the print media who came from outside the Gold Coast were Nnamdi Azikiwe of Nigeria, who later became Governor-General of Nigeria, and Wallace Johnson of Sierra Leone.

The Building of a Launching Pad

Ten years before independence, its launching pad was built. On August 4, 1947, George Grant (Paa Grant) founded the United Gold Coast Convention in Saltpond. That date marked the 50th anniversary of the founding of the Aborigines' Rights protection Society of which Grant was a member. As President of the Convention, he was supported by eight resolute founder-members: E. Ako Adjei, Edward Akufo-Addo, William Ofori Atta (Paa Willie), F. Awoonor-Williams, R. S. Blay, J.B. Danquah, J.W. de Graft-Johnson and E.O. Obetsebi-Lamptey. At Ako Adjei's suggestion, Kwame Nkrumah came from Britain and replaced de Graft-Johnson as General Secretary in December 1947.

Danquah and Nkrumah: Divergent Visions of the Same Goal

J.B. Danquah was the moving spirit, and Kwame Nkrumah the General Secretary of the UGCC. Danquah had introduced and articulated the slogan: "SELF-GOVERNMENT IN THE SHORTEST POSSIBLE TIME." Nkrumah adopted an abridged version: SELF-GOVERNMENT NOW." It was abridged both in quantum of letters and time-frame. Even as General Secretary, Nkrumah was visibly seen moving away from the course the Convention had charted. He was a man in hurry. Indeed, his impatient years commenced in Manchester, England in 1945 when his passion for African emancipation was fuelled by the support of his cronies in the Pan-African Congress.

He may have been a dreamer but the scope of his vision of freedom included the whole of black Africa. His explosive utterances about the total liberation of Africa and so on, were not mere mobilisation slogans: he meant them. On May 25, 1965 he told Parliament in a presidential message that it was his earnest hope that the Conference of Heads of State held in Accra later in the year, would see the birth of a Union Government of Africa. On June 11, in a casual chat in the gardens of Flagstaff House, he said to Ayensu: "Ayensu, some day I will make you the Secretary-General of the Parliament of Africa." What a thing to say! But Nkrumah was dead serious.

Nkrumah fought for the creation of an African High Command. Everyone knows what role this would have played and would now be playing in conflict resolutions in Africa. African nations have been contributing troops for peace-keeping in Africa. An African High command would have been infinitely better. Nkrumah's vision also covered an African Common Market, and African Common Currency, and African Liberation Front, and even an African Olympaid.

Gradually he built the nucleus of his own party. As time passed by, people began to realize that "SELF GOVERNMENT NOW" was not a mere variation on Danquah's theme but the motto of a separate programme which had its own strategy, a programme to be addressed to all, but chiefly to the common man, the 'veranda boy", the chap who had no bedroom. The development drove a wedge between the UGCC and Nkrumah's drawing board party; in practical terms, between Danquah and Nkrumah. It foreshadowed the emergence of the Convention People's Party as a political party within the convention. In previous month Nkrumah had launched the CPP in Saltpond, the home of UGCC. The use of the word "Convention" in the name of Nkrumah's own party is interesting, and possibly significant.

After Nkrumah had launched the CPP, his political appeal hit secondary schools, particularly in Cape Coast. His imprisonment so galvanised the students of Adisadel, Saint Augustine's and Mfantsipim that many went on strike to express their protest. The colonial authorities were unhappy when they sensed that Nkrumah, even behind bars, was proselytising students. As expected, the die-hard students lost their enrolment. That was the signal for the founding in July 1948 of Ghana National college of Cape Coast. It was established in S.O.S circumstances with an unbelievably paltry sum offered by the Founder, Kwame Nkrumah, who had little money. A number of masters on the staff of schools got heavily involved in the pro-Nkrumah movement. When they were dismissed, they went to teach at the new school.

Grant, Danquah and Nkrumah – Their Memorials
George Grant inaugurated the UGCC, but died in 1956 before his dream was realised. After their split, both Danquah and Nkrumah persevered in their separate endeavours. Danquah's working tool was his pen. Blake would have said Danquah did not cease from mental fight nor did his pen sleep by his side. Even out of the depths of solitary confinement, he wrote poignant letters to Nkrumah. Nkrumah's working tool was his

tongue. With it he impetuously proclaimed: "SELF GOVERNMENT NOW". He prodded the "suffering masses" into autosuggesting that their hunger for nationhood would be satisfied by the manna and nectar which only his slogan could provide. Out of empathy, nectar which only his slogan could provide. Out of empathy, Nkrumah gave the name "suffering masses" to the underprivileged, and identified himself and his close associates with them. William Ofori Atta later referred to himself facetiously as a "suffering mass".

Nkrumah did not have the infrastructure which the UGCC had installed. So from its springboard he leapt and landed on ground that was firm enough for him to get on his mark, get set and go. In a moment he was off like a shot. He ran the race of his life. His ears must have tingled with Paul's words: "Know ye not that they which run in a race run all, yet one winneth the prize?" A man of destiny, perhaps, he breasted the tape, setting a world record which was, and still is, acclaimed universally.

"There is a tide in the affairs of men which, taken at the flood, leads on to fortune." Surely it was Paa Grant who in 1947 took the current when it served. In his exhortation on praising great and famous men, William Tarrant says:

> "Praise we wise and brave and strong,
> Who graced their generation;
> Who helped the right and fought the wrong,
> And made our folk a nation."

Danquah has a memorial. Nkrumah has a memorial. Is there a saddening quiet about Grant?

Tragedy of the Crossroads

It is a stubborn fact of history that independence, although it was on course (even if sailing on a slow boat), was catapulted into top gear by the Tragedy of the Crossroads. On February 28, 1948 six months after the inauguration of the UGCC, a group of demobilised soldiers of the Second World War proceeded to march to the Castle to present a petition on their grievances to the Governor. On reaching the Crossroads, that is the junction of the Osu Road and Castle Drive, the Police attempted to halt them. They refused to turn back and three of their number were shot dead by a British officer.

Catching the ex-servicemen's anger and grief, the people rampaged, looted, took to arson and breached the peace in as many ways as the spirit moved them. The situation got out of hand as the disturbances spread to other towns. British District Commissioners wearing helmets and reading Riot Act could not have dispersed the crowds. The Governor was compelled to import security reinforcements from Nigeria. In the evening of the 29th the sound of gun-fire was still heard.

The Tragedy Compounded by a Boycott
A month before the Tragedy of the Crossroads, Nii Kwabena Bonne III (Osu Alata Mantse) and his Anti-Inflation Committee had led a countrywide boycott of foreign goods (from January 26, 1948). Sir Gerald Creasy, the newly appointed Governor, arriving in January, stepped right on a menacingly large faggot which was ready to be ignited to signal the commencement of the boycott programme. The Crossroads shooting exacerbated the biting effect of the January boycott which was finally amicably settled by dialogue.

Detention of the "Big Six"
The Governor declared a State of Emergency. J.B. Danquah sent a cablegram to the Colonial Office in London reporting the disturbances in harrowing detail, asking for the colonial Government to be handed over immediately to the UGCC, and demanding the appointment of a Commission of Enquiry. The UGCC itself also sent a cablegram, but in more moderate terms. The Governor used his Emergency Powers and caused the detention of E. Ako Adjei, Edward Akufo-Addo, William Ofori Atta, J.B. Danquah, Kwame Nkrumah and E.O. Obetsebi-Lamptey. They came to be called "The Big Six".

Commission of Enquiry and Constitutional Committee
A Commission of Enquiry was appointed in March and it started work in April. It comprised Aiken Watson, Lawyer (Chairman); Dr. Keith Murray, Rector of Lincoln College, Oxford; and A. Dalgleish, a trade unionist. Its terms of disturbances and their underlying causes, and to make recommendations on any matter arising from the enquiry. "The Big Six" were represented at the Commission by Dingle Foot, a British Lawyer.

The Commission dealt with the political, economic and social causes of the unrest, and made far-reaching recommendations. The Colonial Office accepted the Watson Report.

In September the Governor appointed a Constitutional Committee to examine the proposals for constitutional and political reforms made in the Watson Report. The Chairman was Justice Henley Coussey (later Sir Henly). The Coussey Report gave the Gold Coast a constitution under which a measure of self-government would be enjoyed. Kwame Nkrumah called that constitution "bogus and fraudulent". It nevertheless formed the basis of the Legislative Council of 1951 which was constituted 101 years after the first Legislative Council of 1850 (established six years after the Bond of 1844). The general election held on February 8, 1951 was won by CPP after a brilliant campaign led by K.A. Gbeedemah and his band of "prison graduates". The "graduates" wore northern-style caps in mimicry of academic mortar-boards. Nkrumah won his seat in Accra Central, not having registered as a voter; the law did not require that. On February 12, he was released from the Accra Ussher Fort Prison in which he had been held as a result of his declaration of Positive Action. His imprisonment instigated the TUC to call a general strike. On release from prison he was appointed leader of Government Business, a not so glamorous name for Prime Minister. A day after Nkrumah's release, Danquah, in characteristic fashion, wrote to him:

> My dear Kwame,
>
> This is a glad occasion. You have fought the good fight and triumphed for the justice of our cause. Your imprisonment and your release are symbolic of the conquest over imperialism. You may have made mistakes, as even the greatest do, but you have passed through a baptism of fire, a spiritual fire, and you have suffered bodily in the cause of our Motherland.
>
> May God Bless You.
>
> Yours Sincerely,
>
> J.B. Danquah

An Honourable Member At 25

Jacob Kwesi Bart-Plange (popularly known as Kwesi Plange) deserved honourable mention here. Born in Cape Coast in October 1925 he was attracted to politics at an early age. He was one of the masters on the staff of St. Augustine's College who were sacked for participating in pro-Nkrumah strike. He became the first headmaster (acting) of Ghana National College at the age of 22. In 1950 he won a Legislative Council bye-election in Cape Coast and thus became the youngest African in British colonial history to get a seat in theLegislature. He was also the first member of the CPP to enter Parliament. He spearheaded the fight in the Legislative Council to get the voting age reduced to 21. He was elected a member of the 1951 Legislative Council and served as Ministerial Secretary to the Minister of Local Government. He died towards the end of 1951 at the age of 27. The life and times of this African prodigy provoke one to quote this lovely passage from "The Parting" by John Norris:

> "How fading are the joys we dote upon!
> Like apparitions seen and gone.
> But those which soonest take their flight
> Are the most exquisite and strong,
> Like angels' visits, short and bright,
> Mortality's too weak to bear them long."

Antenatal Problems

In 1954 birth pangs began to be felt and not without complications. The National Liberation Movement was launched in Kumasi in August of that year under the chairmanship of Bafour Osei Akoto, senior linguist of the Asantehene. The accent of Kumasi was because the party was formed around cocoa farmers. Ashanti, then including Brong-Ahafo, produced the bulk of the country's cocoa crop. It was felt that the CPP had politicised the Cocoa Marketing Board and the Cocoa Purchasing Company to the disadvantage of Ashanti farmers. Some prominent CPP MPs, notably Joe Appiah, Victor Owusu and R.R. Amponsah, defected to the NLM and became more vociferous than when they were in the CPP. The inability of the CPP to win the 1954 Election overwhelmingly, lent momentum to the NLM. The new party reckoned that working in cahoots with the other opposition parties, it would be able to stop the British Government from handing over independence to the CPP. It underlined the superiority of the opposition in terms of overall support by registered voters. It also suspected the Governor, Sir Charles Arden-Clarke, of being a surrogate for Nkrumah.

The following excerpts from a letter written by J.B. Danquah on May 17, 1955 to Claude Barnett, not only give the object of NLM but also underscore a point the authors have made: that the independence struggle started some 100 years before independence Barnett was the Director of the Associated Negro Press Incorporated of Chicago, and a lover of the Gold Coast. The passages also demonstrate Danquah's spirit of accommodation:

> Dear Mr. Barnett
>
> The National Liberation Movement (NLM) is intended to liberate the country from a black dictator and imperial chicanery. The besetting sin of the imperial news pump from the Gold Coast, without any previous preparation, rose overnight in 1948 or 1950 from nothing to something in colonial politics.
>
> Vixre fortes ante Agamemnona. (Many brave men lived before Agamemnon legendary king of Argos who captured Troy).
> Of the two leading Ofori Attas in politics, William is with me and Aaron is against me. He is at present the Minister of Communications in Dr. Nkrumah's second Ministry. I think he is doing well...
> With my warm regards,
>
> Yours sincerely,
>
> J.B. Danquah.

The Name of the Child and the Date of Birth

It is not unusual for a child to be found a name before it is born. J.B. Danquah had consistently espoused the name Ghana for the nation to be. According to historians Ghana used to be a prosperous empire in the North of Africa dating its origin to times B.C. Its original name. Akana, was corrupted by Arabs to become Ghana.

During the reign of King Obeng Kwame, Ghana was invaded by warlike Arabs who desired to impose Islam on its people. They resisted it and eventually deserted their land. The diaspora brought some of them to the Gold Coast. There was no trace of the Ghana empire by the early part of the eleventh century A.D.

The Bond of 1844 was executed on March 6, and Danquah settled on that date for independence. In a message addressed to the chiefs and people on March 6, 1948, following the Tragedy of the Crossroads, and published in all the local papers under the title. "The Hour of Liberation Has Struck", he said this:

That Treaty was made exactly 104 years ago, on March 6th, 1844. In effect we ask for a freely negotiated Bond of 1948. This is evidence that Danquah too had a revolutionary spirit. He was asking for declaration of independence with British consent, which was different from Ian Smith's Unilateral Declaration of Independence for Southern Rhodesia, now Zimbabwe.

Dispersal of the Post-1954 General Election Clouds

After the CPP had won the 1954 General Election, the NLM and its allies were still in no mood to accept the status quo. The CPP won 55 per cent of the votes cast, but only 32 per cent of the registered voters supported it. The Opposition made representations to the Colonial Office in London. A stalemate was developing. The time came when that Office had to clear the way, once and for all, for "this Gold Coast independence business" to succeed. The conservative Secretary of State for the Colonies, Alan Lennox-Boyd, visited Kumasi, sounded opinion and measured feeling. The NLM opted for an independent federal Ghana. The British Government was not enamoured of federalism, but to clear the air once more, it suggested a general election in 1956, which the CPP said was not fair.

In May, 1956 the Secretary of State tabled his Motion in the House of Commons:

> "If a general election is held, Her Majesty's Government will be ready to accept a motion calling for independence within the Commonwealth passed by a reasonable majority in a newly elected legislature, and then to declare a firm date for attainment of this purpose."

The motion was carried unanimously.

The 1956 General Election having also been won by the CPP, the Prime Minister in August of that year made the following Motion in Parliament: "That this Assembly do authorise the Government of Gold Coast to request Her Majesty's Government in the United Kingdom, as soon as practicable this year, to procure the enactment by the United Kingdom Parliament of an Act to provide for the independence of the Gold Coast as a sovereign and independent state within the Commonwealth."

This Motion, too, was carried unanimously.

On January 25, 1957, Lennox-Boyd came to Accra bearing a draft constitution. At the International Airport he said this to the press:

> "I hope the people of the Gold Coast will do everything in their power to smooth out their differences. And I hope my help can be of some use. I am particularly anxious for things to work out smoothly."

After he had consulted the feuding factions, it was announced that a constitution had been agreed. The CPP were happy. The Opposition were not particularly amused. Kojo Botsio and K.A. Gbedemah, on Nkrumah's behalf, later met Lennox-Boyd in London at his request. They accepted the Colonial Office's late proposal to provide for Regional Assemblies in the draft constitution. They had to, because a refusal would have delayed independence.

The Ghana Independence Act, 1957

On February 7, 1957 the House of Commons passed the Ghana Independence Bill which received the Royal Assent on the same day. The Act made provision for, and in connection with, the attainment by the Gold Coast of fully responsible status within the British Commonwealth of Nations.

The Ghana (Constitution) Order In Council, 1957

On February 22, the Ghana (Constitution) Order in Council was made in the presence of "The Queen's Most Excellent Majesty in Council". For the benefit of constitutional enthusiasts, the Order was made under the powers conferred on the Queen by the

British Settlements Acts, 1887 and 1945 (b), The Foreign Jurisdiction Act, 1890 (c), The Ghana Independence Act, 1957, and all other powers enabling her in that behalf by and with the advice of her Privy Council.

By the Transitional Provisions of the Order in Council, the Members and Speaker of the National Assembly of 1956 would, on March 6, 1957, be deemed to have been duly elected Members and Speaker of the Independence Assembly. The Ministers and Ministerial Secretaries would also be deemed to have duly appointed Ministers and Parliamentary Secretaries in the independence executive. The Independence Parliament would comprise the Queen and the National Assembly whose members would be known as Members of Parliament.

Confrontation: Governor Versus Clerk of Parliament

On February 7, 1957 around noon, and a few hours before the Ghana Independence Bill was passed by the House of Commons, Ayensu took five Bills to the Governor, Sir Charles Arden-Clarke for Assent. The two took the opportunity to discuss protocol in relation to the opening of Parliament on Independence Day. The Governor disagreed with Ayensu's plan to place the Throne in the centre of the Speaker's Dais, the Speaker's Chair on its right, and a seat for the Governor on the left of the Throne. The basis of Ayensu's plan was that the Speaker in his House yielded only to the Queen or her representative. On Independence Day the Queen's Special Representative would supplant the Governor; so the number two position would go to the Speaker. An irate Sir Charles sent Ayensu posthaste to London where a meeting held at Kensington Palace upheld Ayensu's position: the Speaker sat on the right of the Throne on Independence Day.

Arrival of the Queen's Special Representative

As it would not be convenient for the Queen to come to open Parliament in person, she deputed Marina, Duchess of Kent to represent her. She arrived at the International Airport on Saturday March 2, accompanied by her Lady-in-Waiting, Lady Rachel Davidson, sister of Duke of Norfolk, and Philip Hay, her Private Secretary and Comptroller. On the stratocruiser that brought the Duchess was R.A. Butler, British Home Secretary and Lord Privy Seal. The Duchess was met by the Governor and the Prime Minister. The airport was agog with the arrival of foreign delegations. The Governor was determined to make his guest comfortable. As many as 90 new Chevrolet cars placed at their disposal, were shuttling between the airport and their lodging places. (They were all sold to the public as soon as the celebrations were over.) To mark the country's independence, the BOAC stratocruiser was painted in Accra in Ghana's colours.

Rehearsal for the Duchess of Kent
On Sunday Ayensu rehearsed the Duchess quietly at Parliament House (formerly King George V Memorial Hall), and after elevenses suggested a second rehearsal straightaway, to which the Duchess graciously agreed. As soon as she went up the Speaker's Dais, she curtsied to the right and to the left. The Dais was rather small and her "recovery" from the first curtsy virtually landed her in the Speaker's Chair which was then mercifully vacant. Humorously she asked what would have happened if the Speaker had been in the Chair. Ayensu assured her that the Speaker would not have minded it, the country being Ghana.

The Day Before The Day
That was March 5, 1957. The Speaker offered a cocktail party to welcome the Duchess of Ghana at the unusual hour of nine in the evening. The last Sitting of the colonial Parliament was held at eleven that evening. After prayers, a Motion on the Adjournment was moved to enable the Prime Minister make a policy statement. This is what he said:

> "Mr. Speaker:
> We have assembled on this happy occasion to honour the new status of a nation. When the day dawns we shall have left behind us the chains of imperialism and colonialism which have hitherto bound us to Britain. By twelve o'clock midnight, Ghana will have redeemed her lost freedom."

He went on and thanked Britain for the part she had played all those many years, and other countries of their assistance to the Gold Coast. He ended with these words:

> "The future is bright and the country looks forward to independent status with hope and pride, but with befitting humility."

The Deputy Leader of the Opposition, S.D. Dombo, associated himself with the Prime Minister's words, conveying thanks to Britain and other countries for helping Ghana to achieve independence.

The Governor's Message proroguing the Legislative Assembly was read by the Speaker. The Clerk thereupon read the Proclamation proroguing the Parliament of Gold Coast at 11.45 o'clock in the evening of March 5, 1957. Accordingly, Parliament rose at a quarter before midnight precisely.

The Independence Vigil

Meanwhile a multitude had foregathered at the Old Polo Ground opposite Parliament House. They were joined there just before midnight by the Prime Minister and his colleagues, and many others from Parliament House. Nkrumah mounted the specially erected podium together with Kojo Botsio, Archie Casely-Hayford, Krobo Edusei, K.A. Gbedemah and N.A.Welbeck. Midnight struck. The wail of the General Post office siren announced the joyful news of the birth of an independent nation in black Africa. The Union Jack gave way to the Ghana flag, and Ghana's national anthem was played officially for the first time. Nkrumah wept, and he was not alone. Then came his celebrated declaration:

> "At long last the battle has ended, and thus, Ghana your beloved country is free for ever."

How the people felt is better left to one's imagination. The venue of Nkrumah's great Declaration on March 6, 1957 was to become the place of internment of his bones on March 6, 1992. The old Polo Ground was renamed Kwame Nkrumah Memorial Park

The Independence Parliament: March 6, 1957
Members of the Executive and Officers of Parliament

Name	Office
Sir Charles Noble Arden-Clarke	Governor-General and Commander-in-chief (Replaced on November 13, 1957 by the Earl of Listowel)
Hon. Dr. Kwame Nkrumah	Prime Minster
Hon. A. Casely-Hayford	Minister of Communications
Hon K.A. Gbedemah	Minister of Finance
Hon. Kojo Botsio	Minister of Trade and Labour
Hon. J.H. Allassani	Minister of Health
Hon. A.E.A. Ofori-Atta	Minister of Local Government
Hon. N.A. Welbeck	Minister of Works
Hon. E. Ako Adjei	Minister of the Interior
Hon. A. E. Inkumsah	Minister of Housing
Hon. J.B. Erzuah	Minister of Education
Hon. B. Yeboah-Afari	Minister of Agriculture
Hon. Krobo Edusei	Minister without Portfolio
Hon L.R. Abavana	Minister without Portfolio
R. O. Amoako-Atta	Parliamentary Secretary, Communications
E.K. Bensah	Parliamentary Secretary, Finance
P.K.K. Quaidoo	Parliamentary Secretary, Trade and Labour
F.K.D. Goka	Parliamentary Secretary, Health
J.E. Hagan	Parliamentary Secretary, Local Government
Ayeebo Asumda	Parliamentary Secretary, Works
C.T. Nylander	Parliamentary Secretary, Interior
F.Y. Asare	Parliamentary Secretary, Housing
C. de Graft-Dickson	Parliamentary Secretary, Education
E.A. Mahama	Parliamentary Secretary, Agriculture
K. Amoa-Awuah	Parliamentary Secretary, Unattached
John Arthur	Parliamentary Secretary, Unattached
Hon. Kojo Botsio	Leader of the House
Prof. K.A. Busia	Leader of the Opposition

Name	Office
Kofi Baako	Government Chief Whip
B.K. Adama	Opposition Chief Whip
Hon. Sir Charles Emmanuel Quist	Speaker
C.H. Chapman	Deputy Speaker
K.B. Ayensu	Clerk of the National Assembly
J.H. Sackey	Assistant Clerk
J.E.Sagoe	Clerk of Committees
C.A. Lokko	Editor of the Official Report
E.K. Doe	Sergeant-at-Arms

Party Representation: There were as many as six parties represented in the Assembly; Convention People's Party (72); Northern People's Party (14); National Liberation Movement (13); Togoland Congress Party (2); Federation of Youth Organisations (1); Moslem Association Party (1). There was one independent Member. (There were no women).

State Opening of the Independence Parliament: March 6, 1957

For the opening of Parliament the Assembly had been summoned for twenty after nine o'clock in the morning. This odd hour was fixed to enable the Queen's Special representative to enter the Chamber of the House precisely at ten. Representatives of many countries, including the Vice-President of the United States, Richard Nixon, had taken their seats before the Sitting hour. The Speaker's Procession on this occasion followed a longer route. Bringing up the rear, he walked deliberately, carrying his stick. The BBC commentator, Wynford Vaughan Thomas told the world that Sir Emmanuel Quist was walking into the House with "measured tread". When the Speaker assumed the Chair, the opening prayers were said by the Clerk who thereafter read the Proclamation Summoning Parliament.

Wearing a radiant white gown bedecked with pearls, the pearls twinkling and the tiara on her head shimmering in the blinding blaze of cine-camera lights, the Duchess of Kent was conducted into the Chamber by the Speaker. As soon as she went up the Speaker's Dais she curtsied to the right, and then to the left. When she had assumed the Throne, the Clerk read the beautifully calligraphed Letters Patent granted under the royal Sign

Manuel empowering the Duchess to open the First Session of the Parliament of Ghana. They conveyed the Queen's greetings to the Governor, the Speaker, Members of Parliament and the people of Ghana. The Queen described her Special Representative as "our most dear and entirely beloved Aunt, Marina, Duchess of Kent, Lady of the Imperial Order of the Crown of India, Dame Grand Cross of Royal Victorian Order, Dame Grand Cross of Our Most Excellent Order of the British Empire". The letters Patent were granted on February 27, by the Queen herself, signed with her own hand Elizabeth R.

The Prime Minister handed the Speech from The Throne to the Duchess. She read it seated. It began with the Queen's apology for her inability to be present herself. She then referred to the Bond of 1844:

> "One hundred and thirteen years ago a number of chiefs entered into an Agreement to acknowledge the power and jurisdiction of my predecessor, Her Late Majesty Queen Victoria."

After the Speech From the Throne the Duchess read the Queen's Message:

> "I have entrusted to my Aunt the duty to open the First Session of the Parliament of Ghana. My thoughts are with you on this great day as you take up the full responsibilities of independent nationhood, and I rejoice to welcome another new member of our growing Commonwealth family of Nations. The hopes of many, especially in Africa, hang on your endeavours. It is my earnest and confident belief that my people in Ghana will go forward in freedom and justice, in unity among themselves and in brotherhood with all the peoples of the Commonwealth.
>
> May God Bless You all."

The Speaker then read and presented to the Duchess an Address of Thanks which she acknowledged. After this the Duchess handed to the Prime Minister the Constitutional Instruments consisting of the Ghana Independence Act, 1957 and the Ghana (Constitution) Order in Council, 1957. Her duties being completed, the Duchess was conducted out of the Chamber by the Speaker.

When the Speaker resumed the Chair, he announced that messages of goodwill had been received from the British House of Commons, the House of Assembly of Northern Nigeria, the Legislative Council of Guiana and the Supreme Soviet of the U.S.S.R.

The Prime Minister moved:

> "That an humble Address be sent to Her Majesty the Queen on behalf of this House."

In the Address reference was made to these words by Edmund Burke, the British politician:

> "We are on a conspicuous stage and the world marks our demeanour."

The Motion was seconded by the Leader of the Opposition, Prof. K.A. Busia.

In his speech he prayed:

> "that the birth of our country as an independent nation within the British Commonwealth may mean for us also a fresh dedication of our talents to the honest and devoted service of our country and generation."

The Motion was carried.
The House was adjourned *sine die*.
In 75 minutes one of the greatest ever political events in black Africa had taken place in Accra, the capital of an independent nation called Ghana.

A Memorable Occasion for Speaker Quist Opening of the New House of Commons

On October 26, 1950 Sir Emmanuel Quist had the singular honour of attending the ceremonies marking the opening of the new House of Commons (whose destruction during the Second

World War prompted the British Prime Minister, Winston Churchill to say: "An enemy has done this." He was the only African Speaker present, in his capacity as President of the Legislative Council of Gold Coast.

Resignation and Death of Speaker Quist

At the Sitting held on November 14, 1957, before question was put on the Motion for the Adjournment of the House, the Speaker, Sir Emmanuel Quist, made this statement:

> "I have to inform you that I am this day occupying for the last time the Speaker's Chair in this Parliament as I have decided, after mature consideration and for health reasons, to resign the office of Speaker of this House, and I propose to hand to His Excellency the Governor-General in the course of the day, the necessary papers."

The Speaker thanked the Clerk and his assistants, the Prime Minister and his colleagues (Ministers and Backbenchers), the Leader of the Opposition and all Members for their help and co-operation. The Leader of the House, Kojo Botsio, on behalf of the Prime Minister, the Government and all Members, conveyed the feeling of regret with which the Speaker's statement had been received, and wished him good health and happy rest. The Deputy Leader of the Opposition, S.D. Dombo, associated himself with the sentiments of the Leader of the House.

Sir Emmanuel resigned his office after serving Parliament as Speaker continuously from 1949. He was first made a Member of the Legislative Council in 1934, and had gained 15 years experience of parliamentary practice before he was appointed President of the Council. The nation's first Speaker, an officer of considerable knowledge and wisdom, died on February 28, 1959 aged 79, and was buried within 48 hours with state honours.

Election of a New Speaker

On November 15, 1957 the House sat, with the Clerk, K.B. Ayensu, presiding. He read a letter from the Governor general informing him that he had received Sir Emmanuel Quist's letter resigning the office of Speaker. He announced that Members would proceed to the election of another Speaker in accordance with the Constitution.

A.M. Akiwumi was elected unopposed. He was conducted into the chamber and upon submitting himself to the will of the House, took and subscribed the Oath of Allegiance and the Speaker's Oath of Office. He was placed in the Chair and the Mace was placed upon the Table. After the Clerk had said the opening prayers, the Speaker was congratulated by the Minister of Justice, E. Ako Adjei, and M.K. Apaloo, an Opposition Member. The Speaker then made his Speech of Acceptance.

Resignation of Deputy Speaker Chapman

The Deputy Speaker, C.H. Chapmen, having resigned his office upon accepting a ministerial appointment, another Member was due to be elected in his place. J.R. Asiedu and Yakubu Tali (Tolon-Na) having both been nominated, the House proceeded to elect J.R. Asiedu by secret ballot.

Preparation for the Establishment of Regional Assemblies

As Clerk of Parliament, Ayensu went to Britain in July 1957 for six weeks to study county council administration in the Greater London Council and the Norwich County Council.

The Inter-Parliamentary Union

Sponsored by the British Parliament, the Parliament of Ghana was admitted to the Inter-Parliamentary Union in 1958. Like the United Nations Organisation, the I.P.U. is an international body. It is open to parliaments of sovereign nations. Founded in 1888, it has its headquarters in Geneva, Switzerland. Like the U.N., the I.P.U. also endeavours to promote international peace. It discusses a wide range of matters including education, health and economics.

The 1958 Plenary Session of the 147th Conference was held in Rio de Janeiro, Brazil at the end of July. As a member-state, Ghana made its debut at that conference. The delegation as originally selected consisted of two CPP MPs. After a hard fight by the Clerk's Office, an Opposition MP was added to the number. The Clerk of Parliament accompanied the delegation as its secretary. He also attended a session of the Association of Secretaries-General of Parliaments, which is an organisation within the I.P.U. The authors mention this particular conference because of the fuss the Brazilians made about the inclusion of an

Opposition MP in the delegation. Nkrumah, who had brought independence to Ghana in 1957, had allowed an Opposition MP to join the delegation? As far as they were concerned, Ghanaians were the most civilised people.

The Commonwealth Parliamentary Association

Ghana's parliament belongs to the Commonwealth Parliamentary Association which groups sovereigns parliaments within the Commonwealth. Its headquarters are in London. Like the I.P.U., it holds an annual conference. A sub-association of the C.P.A. is the Association of Clerks of Commonwealth Parliaments.

The Preventive Detention Act, 1958

This law was enacted in July 1958 and received the Governor-General's Assent in the same month. Under the law, the Governor-General could order the detention of any citizen if he was satisfied that it was necessary to prevent that person from acting in a manner prejudicial to:
   a. the defence of Ghana
   b. the relations of Ghana with other countries, or
   c. the security of the State.

Consisting of only five sections, the Act was inimical to human rights and freedoms. It was as loathsome as it was dreaded. Its semblance of regularity concealed its hidden purpose which was generally suspected before the law was passed. It was subjected to unspeakable abuse. Frontline opponents of the ruling party were either detained or fled the country in fear. More than any other action of the CPP, the Act poured scorn on the party that led the country to independence.

By an irony of fate, some of the party's Pukka Sahibs, both in and outside Parliament, who passionately supported the passage of the law, were years later caught in its fine mesh.

Nkrumah defended the Act: evil-minded persons were being kept away from society by virtue of an Act of Parliament. From his standpoint, doing that by law was better than doing the same thing either on the authority of the scribbled chit, or word of mouth.

Presentation of a Speaker's Chair to Parliament
On February 20, 1959 a Speaker's Chair was presented to Parliament by the House of Commons. A delegation of two Ministers, two backbenchers and an Assistant Clerk made the presentation at the Bar of the House, and the Chair was carried to the Speaker's Dais by the Prime Minister and some of his Ministers.

Aftermath of the Deportation Orders of October 20, 1958
On October 20, 1958 four non-Ghanaians were deported. The orders were signed by the Minister of the Interior, Krobo Edusei and executed by the Commissioner of Police, E.R.T. Madjitey. Following the filing of a writ by J.B. Danquah, the High Court on December 23, 1958 held the two gentlemen to be in contempt of it. The judge however ordered a stay of execution until the following day.

Parliament had been adjourned *sine die* on December 19. It was summoned in emergency circumstances, for December 24, at a quarter after eight o'clock in the morning. Its business was to pass the Deportation (Indemnity) Bill, 1958, taking it through all its stages at the same Sitting. A Certificate of Urgency was laid on the Table for that purpose. The Bill was duly passed and the House adjourned at ten before nine that morning. The High Court was expected to sit at nine.

The Constituent Assembly and Plebiscite Act, 1960
This Act which received the Governor-General's Assent on February 20, 1960 provided for a Constituent Assembly and for the holding of plebiscite on matters relating to the establishment of the Constituent Assembly, with full power to enact such provisions for the framing of a new constitution as it thought fit, including provisions for the establishment of Ghana as a republic. Significantly, the Act was No. 1 of 1960.

Kwame Nkrumah and the Importance of Legal Cover
Nkrumah's zeal for legal cover makes fascinating study. This may have been inborn: he attempted to study law when he went to Britain. But more probably, its was planted by his great admirer, Geoffrey Bing, some time Labour Member of the House of Commons who was his legal advisor. Bing, who served as

Attorney-General for a period, had a sharp mind and was quick on the draw. He and Ayensu consulted quite often in the latter's home. He thought and spoke best when he was on his feet. He would pace up and down, listening, talking, nodding and saying "yes, yes, yes". Out of the profundity of his mind, he conceived legal cover for whatever scheme Nkrumah proposed.

As far as the structure of the public services within the State was concerned, Nkrumah was an iconoclast. By law he replaced the Public Services Commission with Civil Service Commission. By law, he abolished the latter and gave its functions to the Establishment Secretariat, for the better control of which he appointed a Minister of State for Establishment, aided by a Parliamentary private Secretary. By law he became the appointing officer for all categories of judges. By law he set up Special Courts.

Nkrumah's obsession with legal cover was highlighted by the following incident. When a Special Court trying Tawiah Adamafio, E. Ako Adjei and Cofie Crabbe for treason found them not guilty and discharged them, his fury goaded him to ask that Parliament should pass a law to reverse the court's decision. In the end wise counsel prevailed and Nkrumah discharged the residue of his fury by revoking the appointment of the President of the Special Court who happened to be the Chief Justice, Sir Arku Korsah. This took place on December 11, 1963.

When in connection with the four executed deportation orders the Minister of the Interior, Krobo Edusei and the Commissioner of Police E.R.T. Madjitey got into trouble with the law, Nkrumah was careful to avoid a confrontation with the High Court. Instead, he had recourse to an Act of Parliament. The Court had held the two gentlemen to be in contempt of it, but the judge granted a 24-hour stay of execution to facilitate a possible purge of the contempt. That was on December 23. The next day, Parliament was summoned for a quarter after eight o'clock in the morning. Within 35 minutes it had risen, having passed an indemnity law to save the two gentlemen from punishment. A purist may accuse Nkrumah of shielding the two gentlemen but, for him, using legal means to protect them was better than the courts being frustrated by police intervention.

Nkrumah's recourse to retroactive legislation was superlative. Retroactive legislation is making a law today and letting it take effect from the past date. This type of legislation is universally regarded as unprincipled and offensive to the moral law. It is now virtually outlawed by the Constitution.

Nkrumah Presses on the Goal

With the detention law firmly on the statute book, Nkrumah's impatience began to ferment. No one was going to be allowed to disturb any part of his grand design for Ghana: from independence to a republic; from a republic to a one-party state. The detention of J.B. Danquah, Leader of the Opposition, did not upset him. He took the position that Danquah had been detained for perfectly good reasons, and he stoutly defended that position when Ayensu pleaded with him quite often, face to face in Nkrumah's Flagstaff House Office. Nkrumah felt that the coincidence of Danquah and Ayensu marrying two sisters had obviously afflicted Ayensu with mawkishness. Danquah died in the Nsawam Prison on February 4, 1965.

Danquah's working tool, that is his pen, did not sleep by his side. Twelve days before he died he wrote lengthily to Nkrumah. Danquah's wife, visiting him in prison on January 12, 1965, had told him he would have been released on Christmas eve along with William Ofori-Atta and other, but his name had been struck off the list of those to benefit from an amnesty, probably because of the letters he had written to Nkrumah which the latter regarded as annoying. In his last letter to Nkrumah (written 12 days before his death) he tried to explain that it was far from his intention to annoy him. In his accustomed style he made meticulous references to previous letters which had not been answered. An unchanged man, incapable of exuding hate and rather revelling in assuring friends and opponents alike of his highest consideration at all times, he ended his letter in this fashion:

> "And with my warm regards believe me to be, Your Excellency,
> Yours very sincerely and obediently,
> J.B. Danquah."

It was no secret that Nkrumah did not like the multiple-party system of government. As a propaganda gimmick the slogan "Ghana is the CPP, and the CPP is Ghana" was much vaunted.

Nkrumah was already, under the Republic, addressing MPs in Parliament as "comrades" in the socialist sense. The statements he made in the House contained references to "the party" and "our party", although there were then more than one. N.A. Welbeck's official designation in the Parliament was "Minister of Information and Party Propaganda Secretary". Indeed as far as Nkrumah was concerned, the on-party state had been achieved, bar the enactment of the appropriate law. Nkrumah asked the people to support the one-party state and they did so in a referendum. The Constitution was amended and Nkrumah's dream was realised.

Lessons from the Past
The path of true parliamentary democracy is strewn with vexation; "the law's delay, the insolence of office"; government and opposition often in a tug of war; consensus not always emerging. The temptation to dispense with this admittedly difficult form of government is real. An unencumbered alternative is what may be called *Kasapreko* i.e. Speak once (or, When I speak no one else does).

Actually, one-party rule is alien to the country's traditional system of government. However powerful a chief may be, he is meant to be a democrat, not a despot. He should rule with the advice of his elders who take their seats in the Court before he arrives. If he goes off course, he will soon sense the displeasure of his people. If he insists on being an unrepentant ruler, he will face charges which, if proven, will cost him his stool or skin. On the other hand, a head of Government feels secure in the knowledge that to push him out by constitutional means is not so easy. That is why since independence, the three constitutional governments, which have all been thrown out, have been made "to suffer the slings and arrows of outrageous fortune".

Late in the life of the First Republican Parliament (1960-1965), Nkrumah and his associates knew that an undesignated opposition group had established itself within the ranks of the CPP in the House. Its members criticised government measures without disguise, without dread. The astute leader must have seen what the moving finger was writing, but did not want to retreat from his one-party goal. It must be remembered that the country's leaders are human and will listen if the people have the courage to talk to them. Nkrumah once wanted something done in the Old Parliament House for which he had received full political support. When in answer to a question Ayensu, as a Clerk of the House, expressed his opposition, Nkrumah abandoned the project. All that Ayensu suffered in consequence was to be addressed by Nkrumah as "Mr. Opposition".

The CPP presbyters were aware that the one-party state concept had not in fact gained wide acceptance. The popular will expressed in a referendum is not an indication of the personal will. The MP who votes as his Chief Whip desires him to do not express his personal will. When there is talk about the voice of men being the voice of God, what is meant is the free voice of the people. If there is no dialogue between the people and their leaders, trouble brews. This kind of communication-phobia, combined with deceit and flattery is the bane of Ghana's political existence. "The fault ... is not in our stars, but in ourselves that we (in our own sad estimation) are underling."

There is a particular act of moral turpitude which observers will highlight and not palliate. This is what one may call the game of aid and abet and jump aside. A leader decides upon a move which the men in his inner circle perceive to be dangerous. Afraid to stop him, they aid and abet its execution. When a problem arises they anxiously resort to Naaman's act of contrition:

> "In this thing the Lord pardon thy servant, that when my master goeth into the house of Rimmon to worship there, and he leaneth on my hand, and I bow myself in the house of Rimmon, the Lord pardon thy servant in this thing."

Vengeance belongs to God, but sometimes the people audaciously usurp it and wreak it with surprising venom.

The First Women Members of Parliament

Kwame Nkrumah wanted the Republican Parliament to have women in it. To achieve this the Government introduced the Representation of the People (Women Members) Bill in June 1960. It was passed and the Act received the Governor-General's Assent on the 16th of that month.

In moving the Second Reading of the Bill, the Minister of

Local Government, A.E.A. Ofori Atta, said that with the rapid social, economic and political advancement of Ghana, it was necessary that women should play an increasingly important and active role in the government of the country.

The Act made provision for ten extra seats to be created in Parliament for women. Three seats were allocated for the Northern Region, two for the Eastern Region, and two for the Western Region, and one each for the Ashanti, Brong-Ahafo and Volta Regions. Candidates were to be elected by Members of Parliament.

On June 28, the Speaker announced that the following ten women had be returned unopposed in the regions indicated.

Susanna Al-Hassan	-	Northern
Ayanori Bukari	-	Northern
Victoria Nyarko	-	Northern
Sophia Doku	-	Eastern
Mary Koranteng	-	Eastern
Grace Ayensu	-	Western
Christiana Wilmot	-	Western
Comfort Asamoah	-	Ashanti
Lucy Anin	-	Brong-Ahafo, and
Regina Asamany	-	Volta

They were all members of the CPP. On June 28 and 29, they took and subscribed the Oath of Allegiance and the Oath of a Member of Parliament.

An interesting feature of this Act was that if any of the ten seats became vacant, it could not be filled through a bye-election. This special way of getting women into Parliament was not meant to be repeated.

Resignation of Speaker Akiwumi

At the Sitting of Parliament held on June 29, 1960 the Speaker, A.M. Akiwumi announced that the Constitution (Consequential Provisions) Act enacted that day provided that the tenure of office of certain persons, including himself, should come to an end at the commencement of the Act. He was therefore taking the oppoortunity to take leave of the House. He thanked Members for their co-operation and promised his continued interest in the House.

Parliament and the "African Personality"
When it was decided that Ghana would become a republic, the idea occurred to some that under the status, the people should be seen to have moved away from "Westminstry" by the addition of some local touches in Parliament. Kwame Nkrumah's concept of the "African Personality" was still very embraceable. Ayensu suggested a new Mace in the form of a linguist's staff, embossed with suitable adinkra symbols and having for its capital a heraldic bird. Because it would take the form of a linguist's staff, the Mace would rest erect at the north end of the Table and not horizontally on it. When the House was in Committee of the Whole, the existing Mace was placed below the top of the Table. The capital of the new one would in that circumstance be tilted towards the west. Kofi Antubam, the late celebrated artist, chose the adinkra symbols and arranged them. Stapley, the London tutor/goldsmith who wrought the new in silver and gilded it, suggested modifications with which Antubam agreed. An artist's impression was sent to Ghana and approved, and the Mace arrived in Accra on June 15, 1960.

Regarding seating for MPs, the existing arrangement was two sets of benches in the north and south, facing each other. Ministers sat in front in the north, while "Shadow" Ministers sat in front in the south. The term "Backbenchers" derives from the arrangement of the benches conjured up an atmosphere of belligerency. A horse-shoe arrangement would be benign, and that arrangement was in place for the Republican Parliament. The arrangement of seats in the new Parliament House is like the horseshoe, except that the heel end is obtuse. Customs die hard, and even today some MPs refer to the other group as "The Members opposite". The correct phrase is "The Members on the other side."

The Day Before REPUBLIC DAY
On June 30 1960 the last Sitting of the Independence parliament was held. After prayers the Prime Minister moved this Address to be delivered to the Governor-General, the Earl of Listowel:

> "We the Speaker and Members of the National Assembly of Ghana in Parliament assembled wish to tender to Your Excellency the expression of our sincere appreciation and

devotion with which you have served Ghana.

On the eve of Ghana becoming a republic, it is fitting that we should reflect on our association with the Queen and pay our respects to Your Excellency as the last Governor-General and Commander-in-Chief.

We wish Your Excellency good health and much happiness in the future."

The Leader of the Opposition, S.D. Dombo, in seconding the Address, associated himself with the sentiments and wishes expressed by the Prime Minister. The Address was agreed to.

The Governor-General was received at the Bar of the House by the Speaker who conducted him to the Throne. The Prime Minister handed to the Governor-General The Speech From The Throne which he proceeded to read:

"Mr. Speaker and Members of the National Assembly, I come to prorogue this Parliament and to bid you all farewell. By midnight the Monarchy of Ghana will cease and a new republic will be born. It is a tribute to the genius of the people of Ghana that this transition, so often in the past accomplished after bloodshed, bitterness and revolution, has taken place in Ghana with the utmost goodwill, without recrimination, and in accordance both with the letter and with the spirit of the present Constitution."

He said that in a plebiscite held in April in respect of the candidatures of J.B. Danquah and Kwame Nkrumah for the presidency of the republic, the people had chosen Nkrumah. He thanked the Government of Ghana for choosing him as the Representative of The Crown. He wished the president-elect of the Republic and the people of Ghana the utmost good fortune and prosperity in the future. He thanked all who had shown kindness to him and his wife.

The Governor-General then read the Queen's Message:

"From midnight tonight I shall cease to be your Queen. In one sense this is the end of an old association which began just over one hundred and twenty-six years ago when, on behalf of my great great grandmother, the late Queen Victoria, Governor Maclean signed the Bond of 1844.

This formal relationship, thus began, gradually developed until Ghana became in March 1957 a fully independent nation of which I was Queen."

She said that the bonds which bind the Commonwealth could not be expressed in written constitutions or by a set and unchanging formula of relationship. She was proud she was head of a Commonwealth in which every nation might choose for itself the form of government which best suited it. Ghana becoming a republic would not affect the interest which she had always taken in the welfare of its people. The Message continued:

"I have heard from my husband of the sincerity and warmth with which you greeted him on the occasion of his recent visit. I am looking forward with the keenest pleasure to the visit which we shall both pay you next year when I shall come to you as Head of the Commonwealth. On this last occasion when I shall have the opportunity of addressing you as your Queen, I wish to convey to the President, the Members of the National Assembly and the people of Ghana my best wishes for the future. I pray that the blessing of Almighty God may guide the destinies of the new republic and secure peace and happiness for its people."

When the Governor –General had finished speaking, the Prime Minister presented him with the Address which the House had earlier approved, and the Governor-General received it with thanks.

The Governor-General left the Chamber conducted by the Speaker. When the Speaker resumed the Chair, the Clerk read the Governor-General's Proclamation proroguing Parliament at the close of business that day.

The House then rose.

The First Parliament of The First Republic: July 2, 1960

Members of The Executive and Officers of Parliament

Name	Office
H.E. Osagyefo Dr. Kwame Nkrumah	President and Commander-in-Chief
Hon. K.A. Gbedemah	Minister of Finance and Minister of State for Presidential Affairs
Hon. Kojo Botsio	Minister of Foreign Affairs
Hon. E. Ako-Adjei	Minister of Food and Agriculture
Hon. A.E. Inkumsah	Minister of the Interior
Hon. Krobo Edusei	Minister of Transport and Communications and Minister of State for State Ceremonies
Hon. Kofi Baako	Minister of State for Establishment and Presidential Matters in Parliament
Hon. E.K. Bensah	Minister of Works and Housing
Hon. P.K.K. Quaidoo	Minister of Social Welfare
Hon. C. de Graft-Dickson	Minister of Defence
Hon. F.K.D. Goka	Minister of Trade
Hon. R.O. Amoako-Atta	Minister of Labour and Co-operatives
Hon. A.J. Dowuona-Hammond	Minister of Education
Hon. Kwaku Boateng	Minister for Information and Broadcasting
Rev. S.A. Dzirasa	Minister Resident in Guinea
O. Owusu Afriyie	Regional Commissioner, Ashanti
F.Y. Asare	Regional Commissioner, Volta
A. Asumda	Regional Commissioner, Upper
J.E. Hagan	Regional Commissioner, Central
E.H.T. Korboe	Regional Commissioner, Eastern
E. A. Mahama	Regional Commissioner, Northern
S.W. Yeboah	Regional Commissioner, Brong-Ahafo
E.K. Dadson	Parliamentary Secretary
A.K. Onwona-Agyeman	Parliamentary Private Secretary, Finance
A.S.A. Abban	Parliamentary Private Secretary, Agriculture

Name	Office
Kwaku Bonsu	Parliamentary Private Secretary, Justice
J. Kodzo	Parliamentary Private Secretary, Health
A.K. Puplampu	Parliamentary Private Secretary, Foreign Affairs
W.A. Amoro	Parliamentary Private Secretary, Interior
E.I. Preko	Parliamentary Private Secretary, Transport and Communications
W.K. Aduhene	Parliamentary Private Secretary, Establishment and Presidential Matters in Parliament
K.O. Thompson	Parliamentary Private Secretary, Works and Housing
R. Darko-Sarkwa	Parliamentary Private Secretary, Trade
A. Mate Johnson	Parliamentary Private Secretary, Labour and Co-operatives
J. Benibengor-Blay	Parliamentary Private Secretary, Information and Broadcasting
Hon. J.R. Asiedu	Speaker
Yakubu Tali (Tolon-Na)	Deputy Speaker
K.B. Ayensu	Clerk of Parliament
L.P. Tosu	Deputy Clerk
J.H. Sackey	Assistant Clerk
C.A. Lokko	Editor of he Official Report

Party Representation: Convention People's Party (100); United Party (12). (There were ten women)

First Sitting of the First Parliament of the First Republic

The House sat on July 2, 1960 with the Clerk, K.B. Ayensu, presiding. After prayers, the Members present took and subscribed the Oath of Allegiance to the Republic of Ghana which had been proclaimed the previous day. Joseph Richard Asiedu was elected Speaker. He was conducted into the chamber where he submitted himself to the will of the House. He took and subscribed the Oath of Allegiance and the Speaker's Oath. When he was placed in the Chair, he made his Speech of Acceptance.

The House was adjourned till the next day.

State Opening of the First Parliament of the First Republic: July 5, 1960

At nine o'clock in the morning, in the presence of numerous foreign delegations and distinguished guests, the House commenced proceedings.

After the usual formalities the President, Dr. Kwame Nkrumah, was conducted into the Chamber to the sound of fontomfrom (state drums) and mmensuon (the seven state horns), a break with the days when fanfare was sounded by army trumpeters.

The President delivered The Sessional Address:

> "Mr. Speaker, Honourable Members: Four days ago the nation was ushered into a new life by the proclamation of the Republic of Ghana. Today the first formal meeting of Republican Parliament takes place in changed circumstances, both in regard to physical arrangements of the House and the spirit of excitement which possesses us at this moment. By the voluntary act of our people we have chosen the path we wish to tread.
>
> Mr. Speaker, We of this generation must reflect on the extraordinary good fortune we have enjoyed. We do not merely live in exciting times. We are creating the history of our nation as we translate into practical reality the dreams and visions of our forefathers.
>
> Mr. Speaker, Members of Parliament, in the earnest hope that divine providence may guide your deliberations and further the welfare of our people, I now leave you to the successful discharge of your duties."

The President departed.

The House adjourned at five after ten o'clock in the morning. The proceedings of this long-awaited day lasted only 50 minutes.

The Last Sitting of the First Parliament of the First Republic

This was held on May 25, 1965. The Leader of the House (then Kofi Baako) delivered a message from The President. The Message embodied a review of the First Parliament of the First Republic:

"In a socialist society the welfare of the workers is synonymous with the welfare of the State. For this reason the Government have, by their legislative enactments during the past five years, underlined the unique position of the workers in our society and the need to adopt such policies as would promote their welfare and protect them against capitalist exploitation.

As the House is aware, the Government have set up under the Statutory Corporations Act, a large number of corporations and state enterprises during the life of this Parliament, to relieve the country of too much dependence upon foreign commercial and industrial concerns which tended to have strangulating effect on our economy. For the same reason the establishment of the Bank of Ghana and the Ghana Investment Bank by statutes passed during this Parliament's life, have accelerated the pace of banking for commercial and economic purposes. Recently, Parliament enacted the Social Security Act, 1965 which has established another milestone in our onward march towards a socialist society.

One of the greatest achievements of this Parliament has been enactment of such legislation as would protect the nation against saboteurs from within and without. For this reason, the Preventive Detention Act of 1958 has been strengthened by the amending Acts of 1962 and 1963, to increase the security of the State against those who would stop short of nothing to jeopardize the country's orderly progress by resorting to violent methods to achieve their selfish political ambitions.

The people of Ghana have great opportunity later this year to play host to the Conference of Heads of State and Government of the Organisation of African Unity in Africa.

It is my earnest hope that this Conference will see the birth of a Union Government of Africa."

The message was followed by a number of Members speaking in praise of the President whom they affectionately and variously described as "Osagyefo" "Our Great Leader", "The Father of the Nation". The Minister of Parks and Gardens, E.N. Ocansey took the cake when he rose and made a speech of seven words: "Mr. Speaker, I say Praise God, Hallelujah!"

The President was then conducted into the Chamber where he delivered The Dissolution Address. He informed the House that the membership of the next Parliament would be increased from 114 to 198 as recommended by the Delimitation Commission. He said that to ensure that MPs faithfully discharged their responsibilities and obligations to their constituents, the Central Committee of the Party would be empowered by law to unseat any Member who, in the opinion of he Central Committee, had lost the confidence of the Party.

The President departed.

The Clerk read the Proclamation dissolving Parliament. The House was adjourned sine die.

Highlights of the First Parliament of the First Republic

The most sensational achievement was the emergence of that Parliament out of the creation of a one-party state. The other highlights were enunciated in the review of that Parliament presented to the House at its last Sitting held on May 25, 1965

The Second Parliament of the First Republic: August 24, 1965

Members of the Executive and Officers of Parliament

Name	Office
H.E. Osagyefo Dr. Kwame Nkrumah	President and Commander-in-Chief
Hon. Kojo Botsio	Chairman, State planning Commission
Hon. N.A. Welbeck	Minister of State for Party Propaganda
Hon. Imoru Egala	Minister of Industries
Hon. L.R. Abavana	Minister of the Interior
Hon. Kofi Baako	Minister of Defence
Hon. E.K. Bensah	Minister of Works
Hon. A.J. Dowuona-Hammond	Minister of Communications
Hon. Kwaku Boateng	Minster of Science and Higher Education
Hon. O. Owusu-Afriyie	Minister of Health
Hon. K. Amoako-Atta	Minister of Finance

Name	Office
Hon. B.A. Kwaw-Swanzy	Minister of Justice and Attorney-General
Hon. F.A. Jantuah	Minister of Agriculture
Hon. Alex Quaison-Sackey	Minister of Foreign Affairs
Hon. Kwesi Armah	Minister of Trade
Hon. Dr. Ekow Daniels	Deputy Attorney-General
Hon. J.E. Hagan	Regional Commissioner, Central
Hon. S.W. Yeboah	Regional Commissioner, Western
Hon. Ayeebo Asumda	Regional Commissioner, Upper
Hon. R.O. Amoako-Atta	Regional Commissioner, Ashanti
Hon. Joseph Kodzo	Regional Commissioner, Volta
Hon. Ebenezer Adam	Regional Commissioner, Northern
Hon. H.S.F. Provencal	Regional Commissioner, Greater Accra and Executive Chairman, Special Commissioner Accra-Tema City Council
Hon N. Anane-Adjei	Regional Commissioner, Brong-Ahafo
Hon. I.K. Chinebuah	Minister of Education
Hon. E.N. Ocansey	Minister of Parks and Gardens
Hon. E.A Mahama	Minister of Animal Husbandry
Hon. Hans Kofi Boni	Minister of Food and Nutrition
Hon. Mumuni Bawumia	Minister of Local Government
Hon. F.E. Tachie-Menson	Minister of Housing
Hon. K. Amua-Awuah	Minister of Labour
Hon. E. I. Preko	Minister of Fuel and Power
Hon. J. Benibengor-Blay	Minister of Arts and Culture
Hon. A.R. Pupulampu	Minister of Lands
Hon. S.A. Kwaku Bonsu	Minister of Pensions and National Insurance
Hon. Mrs. Susanna Al-Hassan	Minister of Social Welfare and Community Development
Hon. K.O. Thompson	Minister of Mines and Mineral Resources
Hon. B.A. Konu	Minister of Fisheries
Hon. I.W. Benneh	Minister of Rural Industries
Hon. J.Y. Ghann	Minister of Information
Hon. Baffour Kwabena Senkyire	Minster of Co-operatives
Hon. B.A. Bentum	Minister of Forestry

Name	Office
Paul Tagoe	First Parliamentary Secretary
A.K. Onwona-Agyeman	Second Parliamentary Secretary
Hon. Kofi Asante Ofori-Attah	Speaker
A.E. Inkumsah	First Deputy Speaker
Alhaji Yakubu Tali (Tolon-Na)	Second Deputy Speaker
Hon. Kofi Baako	Leader of the House
Hon. E.K. Bensah	Deputy Leader of the House
K.B. Ayensu	Clerk of Parliament
L.P. Tosu	Deputy Clerk
A.S. Kpodonu S.N. Darkwa	Assistant Clerks
C.A. Lokko	Editor of Debates
P.O. Quaye	Marshal

For the election of Members to this Parliament, the first in the one-party state, each constituency nominated only one candidate. On May 28, the names of all the 198 candidates were announced on the national radio. At the hour appointed for the close of nominations, all the candidates were returned unopposed. If any constituency had nominated more than one candidate, the electors would have exercised their right to choose. (There were ten women.)

It is remarkable that this administration had as many as 42 ministerial positions and only two parliamentary secretary positions.

First Sitting of the Second Parliament of the First Republic
This was held on June 10, 1965 with the Clerk, K.B. Ayensu, presiding.

After prayers, Kofi Asante Ofori-Atta (formerly A.E.A. Ofori-Atta) was elected Speaker. He was conducted into the Chamber where he submitted himself to the will of the House. He took and subscribed the Oath of Allegiance and the Speaker's Oath. He was placed in the Chair, and thereupon he made his speech of Acceptance. A.E. Inkumsah and Alhaji Yakubu Tali (Tolon-Na) were elected First and Second Deputy Speakers.

Osagyefo Dr. Kwame Nkrumah's nomination as President was approved by the House.

The House was adjourned *sine die*.

State Opening of the Second Parliament of the First Republic: August 24, 1965

After prayers the President was received into the Chamber. The President delivered the Sessional Address. He said, *inter alia:*
"From now on we must devote all our energies to the pursuit of unifying and progressive ideology, a dynamic but flexible economic policy, a positive but constructive role in the African revolution, and a balanced relationship with the rest of the world. Above all we must devote our energies to the establishment of a strong and prosperous socialist society which can fulfil the aims and aspirations of our people. Because the people confirmed the Party's choice in the recent general election, our national assembly has emerged as a consensus between the people and the Party. In this sense, this Parliament is in reality Ghana's first parliamentary expression of a People's Socialist Democracy.

With our adoption of the one-party system of government, this House, this National Assembly of rancour and vituperation were often used by the opposition as weapons to discredit the Government with the aim of overthrowing it. This House has now assumed a new character and atmosphere, and this has made a significant change in the role and conception of the Speaker's Chair. The days are gone when the Speaker sat like an umpire over the dissensions, bickering and parliamentary manoeuvres of rival political parties. Ours is a House united by one party, one ideology, one aim one destiny."

Toward the end of the Sessional Address, the President, for the first time addressed the House thus:

"Mr. Speaker, Members and Comrades of the National Assembly."

The President departed.
The House was adjourned till the following day.

Attendance of the Speaker at the 700th Anniversary Celebrations In London

The Speaker, Kofi Asante Ofori-Atta was elected on June 10. In a week's time he was on his way to London where on June 22, he, with Speakers from all over the Commonwealth attended the ceremonies marking the 700th anniversary (1265-1965) of Simon de Montford's Parliament. This man is regarded as the first proper Speaker of the House of Commons, although Peter de Montford is recorded as having been appointed Speaker in 1258.

The Last Sitting of the Second Parliament of the First Republic

On February 22, 1966 Parliament held a sitting at the unusual hour of eleven in the morning. It was Budget Day and the galleries were full. The Minister of Finance, K. Amoako-Atta, moved his Motion in the following flamboyant terms:

> "Mr. Speaker, By Command of Osagyefo the President, General Secretary and Chairman of the Central Committee of the Party, our Standard-Bearer of the African Revolution, I beg to move That this House approve the Financial Policy of the Government for the year ending 31st December 1966."

The debate on this Motion being postponed till February 28, the House was adjourned till the next day. The debate on the Budget was overtaken by the overthrow of Kwame Nkrumah's Government on February 24. The significance of that day was that it saw the very first coup d'etat in Ghana, and the only one undertaken jointly by the Armed Forces and the Police Service.

Ayensu's personal diary contains these interesting entries for that day and the three previous days. The *dramatis personae* in this play of doom were all associated with the ill fated Parliament of 1965.

Monday February 21:

Nkrumah left for Cairo en route to Hanoi. Kwesi Armah (Minister of Trade), Alex Quaison-Sackey (Minister of Foreign Affairs and a whole lot with him. National Assembly's 13th Sitting began at 12 Noon. ...Didn't go to Kojo Botsio's party to celebrate his 50th Birthday (Botsio then Chairman of the State Planning Commission in Nkrumah's Government).

Tuesday February 22:

National Assembly's 14th Sitting commenced at 11. Full House. Budget Day. Adjourned 2.30 or so.

Wednesday February 23:
No Sitting. ... To Saint Patrick Lodge (Masonic). Kofi Asante Ofori Atta (Speaker) "passed" and "raised". Long ceremony. "Raising" performed by A.E. Inkumsah (First Deputy Speaker) (in presence of K.B. Ayensu, Clerk, and Joe Welsing, Assistant Editor of Debates).

Thursday February 24:
Announced on Radio Ghana that the Military in co-operation with the Police had taken over the Government of Ghana (Nkrumah being in Peking).

Highlights of the Second Parliament of the First Republic

This Parliament, the first in the one-party state, was officially opened on August 25, 1965. It was abrogated on February 24, 1966 i.e. precisely six months after the opening and eight months after the first Sitting when the Speaker was elected.

On December 16, 1965 the President informed Parliament that Ghana had severed diplomatic ties with the United Kingdom over the Southern Rhodesian issue. The independent African states had given the United Kingdom Government an ultimatum that if by December 15, 1965 it had not put down Ian Smith's rebellion in unilaterally declaring Southern Rhodesia independent, they would cut their ties with it.

On December 20, 1965 the House supported the Private Member's Motion proposed by S.I. Iddrissu, asking for the establishment of an African Continental Parliamentary Association open to all sovereign African states. The Association would discuss problems peculiar to Africa and help in bring about African unity.

On February 16, 1966 an unprecedented even occurred. It was announced in the House that S.I. Iddrissu had been unseated, having been expelled from the Party because of disloyalty, on the recommendation of its Central Committee.

Preparation for a Return to Parliament

Under the National Liberation Council, a Constituent Assembly under the speakership of R.S. Blay, an eminent lawyer of Sekondi, adopted and enacted a new Constitution for the Second Republic on August 15, 1969. Before then a Constitutional commission under the chairmanship of Justice Edward Akufo-Addo, Chief Justice, had prepared constitutional proposals. Under that constitution there were a titular Head of State and a Prime Minister. The Prime Minister and all his ministers were to be Members of Parliament.

A general election was held on August 29, 1969. The CPP having been proscribed, did not participate in it. Dr. K.A. Busia and his Progress Party won the election.

The First Parliament of the Second Republic: October 2, 1969

Members Of The Executive And Officers Of Parliament

Name	Office
H.E. Justice Edward Akufo-Addo	President and Commander-in-Chief
Rt. Hon. Dr. K.A. Busia	Prime Minister
Hon. J. Kwesi Lamptey	Minister of Defence
Hon. William Ofori Atta	Minister of Education, Culture and Sports
Hon. R.A. Quarshie	Minister of Trade, Industry and Tourism
Hon. S.D. Dombo	Minister of the Interior
Hon. R.R. Amponsah	Minister of Lands and Mineral Resourses
Hon. K.K. Anti	Minister of Local Administration
Hon. Victor Owusu	Minister of External Affairs
Hon. S.W. Awuku-Darko	Minister of Works
Hon. Jatoe Kaleo	Minister of Labour and Co-operatives
Hon. N.Y.B. Adade	Minister of Justice and Attorney-General
Hon. J.H. Mensah	Minister of Finance and Economic Planning
Hon. G.D. Ampaw	Minister of Health
Hon. T.D. Brodie-Mends	Minister of Information
Hon. Dr. Kwame Safo-Adu	Minister of Agriculture
Hon. Dr. W.G. Bruce-Konuah	Minister of Housing
Hon. A.A. Munufie	Minister of Youth and Rural Development
Hon. Haruna Esseku	Minister of Transport and Communications

Name	Office
Hon. B.K. Adama	Minister of State for Parliamentary Affairs
Hon. K.G. Osei-Bonsu	Minister of State and Chief of State Protocol
Hon. Kwaku Baah	Ministerial Secretary, Interior
Hon. M. Abdul-Saaka	Ministerial Secretary, Defence
Hon. J.A. Kuffuor	Ministerial Secretary, External Affairs
Hon. H.W. Kofi-Sackey	Ministerial Secretary, Works
Hon. O.K. Poku	Ministerial Secretary, Housing
Hon. S. Osei-Akoto Hon. J.W. Manu	Ministerial Secretaries, Transport and Communications
Hon. Dr. Jones Ofori Atta Hon. C.O. Nyanor	Ministerial Secretaries, Finance and Economic Planning
Hon. A.A. Aboagye da Costa Hon. Carl D. Reidorf	Ministerial Secretaries, Youth and Rural Development
Hon. Stephen Krakue Hon. Adam Amandi	Ministerial Secretaries, Trade, Industry and Tourism
Hon. A. Appiah-Menka	Deputy Attorney-General
Hon. A.A. Abedi	Ministerial Secretary, Office of the Prime Minister
Hon. M.K. Osei	Ministerial Secretary, Labour and Co-operatives
Hon. S.K.C. Osei-Baidoo	Ministerial Secretary, National Service Corps
Hon. Shanni Mahama	Ministerial Secretary, Agriculture
Hon. A. Antwi-Kusi Hon. K.P. Agyekum	Ministerial Secretaries, Lands and Mineral Resourses
Hon. J.G. Amamoo	Ministerial Secretary, Health
Hon. S.K. Opon Hon. Oheneba Kwow Richardson	Ministerial Secretaries, Education, Culture and Sports
Hon. Justice Akuamoa Boateng Hon. Dr. J.R. Fynn	Ministerial Secretaries, Local Administration
Hon. B.K. Adama	Leader of the House
Hon. Saki Scheck	Government Chief Whip
Dr. G.K. Agama (later replaced by E.R.T. Madjitey)	Leader of the Opposition
Lydia A. Akanbodiipo	Opposition Chief Whip
Hon. Justice Nii Amaa Ollennu	Speaker
Hon. Isaac Amissah-Aidoo	Deputy Speaker

Name	Office
C.A. Lokko	Clerk of Parliament
S.N. Darkwa J.N. Kudadjier D.S.K. Kanda K.E.K. Tachie E. Pianim	Assistant Clerks
S.D. Dodoo	Editor of Debates

Party Representation: Progress Party (105); National Alliance of Liberals (29); United Nationalist Party (2); United Action Party (2); All People's Republican Party (1); Independent (1). Subsequently the NAL, UNP and APRP merged into the Justice Party. (There were two women).

First Sitting of the First Parliament of the Second Republic

Parliament held its first Sitting in the Conference Hall, State House Complex on September 5th, 1969 with the Clerk, C.A. Lokko presiding.

After prayers, Justice Nii Amaa Ollennu was elected Speaker. He was conducted into the Chamber where he submitted himself to the will of the House. After taking and subscribing the Oath of Allegiance and the Speaker's Oath, he was placed in the Chair. He then made his Speech of Acceptance. Isaac Amissah-Aidoo was elected Deputy Speaker.

Members present took and subscribed the Oath of Allegiance and the Oath of a Member of Parliament.

The House was adjourned *sine die*.

State Opening of the First Parliament of the Second Republic: October 2, 1969

After prayers the Clerk read the Instrument Summoning Parliament.

Brig. A.A. Afrifa, J.W.K. Harlley and Lt. Gen. A.K. Ocran, Chairman and Members of the Presidential Commission inaugurated on September 3, were conducted into the Chamber.

The Chairman delivered the Sessional Address:

> "This day begins another era of parliamentary rule in Ghana. The Government is determined to keep its promise

to the people of this country to achieve for its good government, and the freedoms essential for a happy democratic life. To this end, it will endeavour to establish a democratic welfare society in which, as far as our human and material resources will allow, every citizen will live a life of dignity in freedom.

On 24th February, 1966 Ghana's indebtedness (principal and interest) stood at N₵ 889 million. Since then the National Liberation Council has made repayments totalling N₵220 million. Yet the National Liberation Council has had to borrow more money for viable projects necessary to activate our economy and to provide much needed employment. For this reason or present national indebtedness stands at N₵ 1,003 million, an increase of N₵ 114 million since the coup. It should be noted, however, that N₵ 70 million of this represents aid which has not yet been used. But the stark fact is that we are a nation heavily in debt, with many able bodied men and women unemployed, and a rising cost of living. This is a serious situation. But it was worse when the National Liberation Council overthrew the Convention People's Party regime, and the situation dictated the deflationary economic policy which the Council has had to pursue. The time has now come for the new government to turn to a more expansionist policy. That is why we have decided on the priorities first mentioned. We conceive a steady development aimed at: the general modernisation of rural areas; the bridging of regional disparities; and agricultural expansion as an aspect of rural development."

Brig. Afrifa said immediate attention would be given to agriculture, the production of more food, and reversal of the longstanding tendency towards shortages and high process of basic commodities.

Special attention would be given to the training and employment of youth. The housing programme would be stepped up and the accent placed on the use of local materials. Regarding industries, the Government would ensure the full utilisation of factory capacity. The existing system of administrative regulation of trade will be dismantled soon. Progress towards a liberal regime of imports would be accelerated. The Government would wage war on corruption. The Government would at all times accord respect for the Opposition, and it hoped for reciprocal cooperation. The Leader of the Opposition would receive a salary and be a Member of the Council of State. He concluded thus:

> "Finally, Mr. Speaker, ... The Government will do its best to fulfil their aspirations (those of the NLC, the Armed Forces and the Police) for the nation which inspired their courage, their sacrifice and their exemplary demonstration of magnanimity and greatness."

The Chairman and Members of the Presidential Commission departed.

The House was adjourned till the following day.

Highlights of the Parliament of the Second Republic
In 1970 the Prime Minister, Dr. K.A. Busia ordered the dismissal of 568 public officers in exercise of a power which he believed he had under the 1969 Constitution. This caused tremendous concern among the people, especially as some of the dismissed officers were occupying top positions in the country. A Private Member's Motion deploring this action was defeated by the Government's strength in the House. Edward Sallah, a member of the management of the Ghana National Trading Company challenged the Prime Minister's action in the Supreme Court. The Court ruled that the dismissal of the 568 public officers was unconstitutional. The Prime Minister reacted quite angrily to the Court's ruling and thereby gained the nickname "No Court", a phrase he used in the protest speech. This was an unhappy episode, especially as the Prime Minister's decision to dismiss the public officers was not supported by some of the top guns in his party who were lawyers of stature. One of the Bills introduced by the Government was the Industrial Regulations (Amendment) Bill. The Opposition walked out during its Consideration Stage. It was argued that the overall effect of the Bill was to disestablish the Traders Union Congress by giving workers an unrealistic freedom of association with groups of their choice.

Christmas 1971 fell on a Saturday. Boxing Day was the following day, Sunday; so Monday the 27th was a public holiday.

On that day the Prime Minister took a very bold step, a step meant only for the courageous. He devalued the Cedi by 44 per cent. He told the nation about it in a broadcast and the change in the value of our currency took effect at nine o'clock that evening. Dr. Busia tried to cushion the effect of the devaluation by announcing graduated increases in salaries and wages, and a higher producer price of cocoa. Beer had been rationed in drinking bars over the Christmas holidays. New Year was yet to be celebrated. The timing of the devaluation disfavoured the Prime Minister, and the widespread dissatisfaction with the devaluation provided ammunition for the Armed Forces which overthrew the Government on January 13, 1972.

A Second Preparation for a Return to Parliament

The 1979 Constitution gave the country an American type of government with a single Chamber. It provided for a President with considerable executive powers, and Ministers to be appointed from outside Parliament. It was promulgated by a Constituent Assembly under the chairmanship of Justice V.C.R.A.C. Crabbe, a Judge of the Superior Court of Judicature. As a "blueprint" for that Assembly, a document was prepared by Dr. Thomas Mensah, a distinguished lawyer then at the Commonwealth Secretariat in London.

The general election held in 1979 was won by Dr. Hilla Limann and his People's National Party.

First Parliament of the Third Republic: September 24, 1979

Members of the Executive and Officers Of Parliament

Name	Office
H.E. Dr. Hilla Limann	President and Commander-in-Chief
H.E. Prof J.W.S. de Graft –Johnson	Vice President
Hon. Dr. Amon Nikoi (Later replaced by Hon. Prof. George Benneh)	Minister of Finance
Hon. S.K. Riley-Poku	Minister of Defence
Hon Prof. Ekow Daniels	Minister of the Interior
Hon. Dr. Isaac Chinebuah	Minister of Foreign Affairs
Hon. Francis Dadzie	Minister of Agriculture

Name	Office
Hon. S.K.P. Jantuah	Minister of Local Government, Rural Development and Co-operatives
Hon. Dr. Kwamena Ocran	Minister of Health
Hon. H.R. Sawyerr	Minister of Transport and Communications
Hon Col. David Zanlerigu	Minister of Works and Housing
Hon. F.K. Buah	Minister of Trade and Tourism
Hon. Vincent W. Bullah	Minister of Industries, Science and Technology
Hon. Dr. Edmond Y. Ablo	Minister of Education, Culture and Sports
Hon. Dr. John S. Nabila	Minister of Information and Presidential Affairs
Hon. Joe Reindorf	Minister of Justice and Attorney-General
Hon. Yaw Opoku-Afriyie	Regional Minister, Brong Ahafo
Hon. E.T. Torto	Regional Minister, Greater Accra
Hon. Alhaji Ibrahim Haruna	Regional Minister, Northern
Hon. George Nandzo	Regional Minister, Upper
Hon. Johnson Dado	Regional Minister, Volta
Hon. Sam Cudjoe	Regional Minister, Western
Hon. E.A. Haizel	Regional Minister, Central
Dr. E.L. Nyakotey	Deputy Minister, Finance and Economic Planning
Kankam da Costa	Deputy Minister, Defence
Antwi Nimo	Deputy Minister, Interior
Dr. Yakubu Saaka	Deputy Minister, Foreign Affairs
Dr. K. Gyamfi	Deputy Minister, Agriculture
Mrs. Janet Yirenkyi K.K. Asante	Deputy Ministers, Local Government, Rural Development and Co-operatives
Dr. F.W.A. Akuffo	Deputy Minister, Health
Samuel Nunoo	Deputy Minister, Transport and Communications
Dr. T.A. Donkor Emmanuel Arthur	Deputy Ministers, Works and Housing
Wulff Tagoe Dr. Charles Van Dyck	Deputy Ministers, Lands, Natural Resources, Fuel and Power
A. Bediako	Deputy Minister, Trade and Tourism

Name	Office
Dr. Francis Acquah	Deputy Minister, Industries, Science and Technology
E.K. Tumasi Miss Adisa Mukaila	Deputy Ministers, Labour, Youth and Social Welfare
Dr. Kofi Owusu Bempah	Deputy Minister, Education, Culture and Sports
James Ampah Kwofie	Deputy Minister, Information and Presidential Affairs
S.G. Arthur	Deputy Regional Minister, Brong-Ahafo
J.N. Wussah	Deputy Regional Minister, Greater Accra
A.A. Baba	Deputy Regional Minister, Northern
L.M. Awuni	Deputy Regional Minister, Upper
Daniel Agume	Deputy Regional Minister, Volta
L.T. Ocran	Deputy Regional Minister, Western
Kwesi Dougan	Deputy Regional Minister, Central
Hon. Justice Jacob Hackenburg Griffiths-Randolph	Speaker
Edmond Dramani Mahami	First Deputy Speaker
Leonard Peace Tosu	Second Deputy Speaker
J.E.K. Aggrey-Orleans	Acting Clerk of Parliament
S.N. Darkwa	Deputy Clerk
D.S.K. Kanda	Principal Assistant Clerk
R. Owusu Ansah Abrefa J.S.E. de Graft-Johnson	Assistant Clerks
J.O. Amugi	Acting Editor of Debates

(Note: The list of Ministers, Regional Ministers and Deputy Regional Ministers is as it appears in the Official Report of Parliament for September 25, 1979. it is not complete)

Party Representation: People's National Party (71); Popular Front Party (42); United National Convention (13); Action Congress Party (10); Social Democratic Front (3); Independent (1). (There were five women).

First Sitting of the Parliament of the Third Republic and Inauguration of the Third Republic: September 24, 1979
The House sat, with the Acting Clerk, J.E.K. Aggrey-Orleans presiding.

A distinguished visitor was President Ahmed Sekou Toure of Guinea.

After prayers Justice Jacob Hackenburg Griffiths-Randolph was elected Speaker. He was conducted into the Chamber where he submitted himself to the will of the House. He took and subscribed the Oath of Allegiance and the Speaker's Oath. He was placed in the Chair, whereupon he made his Speech of Acceptance. Edmond D. Mahami and L.P. Tosu were elected First and Second Deputy Speakers.

Members present took and subscribed the Oath of Allegiance and the oath of a Member of Parliament. The Members of the Armed Forces Revolutionary Council, led by their Chairman, Flight Lt. Jerry John Rawlings; the President Elect, Dr. Hilla Limann; and the Vic-President-Elect, Prof. J.W.S de-Graft-Johnson were received into the Chamber.

The President-Elect and the Vice-President-Elect took and subscribed the Oath of Allegiance and the Oath of Office.

The Chairman of the AFRC addressed the House. He said that the AFRC had demonstrated openly that in Ghana the holding of office in government had, in almost all cases, been used to plunder the wealth of the nation. The Suspense Account of the AFRC in Accra alone stood at ¢13 million. On the international scene, Ghana's image had been restored. The offers of aid and co-operation from both East and West, especially from our African brothers, were the legacy the AFRC was leaving for the new administration. The AFRC Chairman said:

> "While inflation was rising, others were dipping their hands freely into the coffers of the State.
>
> "Mr. President, we of the Armed Forces Revolutionary Council have faith in you and your government. We know you will deliver the goods. That is why we have turned a deaf ear to those who have entreated us to stay on a little longer because our job is not complete. We have every confidence that we shall never regret our decision to go back to barracks.
>
> "We wish you good luck, Mr. President, and you too, Honourable Ministers and Members of Parliament that you, Mr. President, you did not chicken out of the election but went ahead to seek representation of your people in

spite of the fact that we were on the scene with plain evidence of our revolutionary intent, suggests you are a man of mettle. Ghana is looking up to you. Thank you."

The Chairman of the AFRC handed a symbolic Scroll of Office to the President.

The President then delivered the Inaugural Address:

"We have convened at a most crucial time in our history which marks the end of long period of blatant and shameless abuses which have so destroyed confidence in our people, in all our institutions and in our values, that we are all yearning for a wholesome change for the better. Never before, since independence have the demands on government therefore been greater, the tasks heavier, and fears, hopes and expectations higher than now. After many years of drift, of wandering in the political and economic wilderness, Ghana is about to find her feet and level again."

The President thanked all Ghanaians for electing him to lead in the bleakest and most uncertain period of the people's lives. He said that the dawn of a new era of peace and hope for progress and stability afforded him the pleasure to extend a special welcome to President Sekou Toure and other distinguished guests. He continued:

"In the name of Dr. Nkrumah and the other founding fathers, we offer another dream again today, the dream of economic recovery and social fulfilment in the years ahead."

President Limann thanked the AFRC for conducting the general elections and organising the activities culminating in the inaugural ceremony.

"I pray for God's guidance and blessing to enable me protect the most precious gift Ghanaians have given me, their confidence, which I accept in all humility and which I shall treasure with all my mind and all my strength, only for as long as I retain their trust. Thank you."

The President, the Vice-President and the outgoing Chairman

and Members of the AFRC departed.
The House was adjourned till the next day.

Highlights of the Parliament of the Third Republic

Question Time was introduced belatedly. During Question Time, the first hour of a Sitting, Ministers answer Private Members' questions, of which notice in writing has been given. It enables MPs to fulfil their investigative functions by way of interpellations, and is a feature of the French and other European parliaments.

Perhaps the most outstanding even in the 1979 Parliament was the rejection of the Budget presented by the Government. It was unprecedented. On July 2, 1981, the Majority Leader, C.C. Fitih, made a Motion asking the House to approve the Financial policy of the Government for the year ending June 30, 1982 as presented by the Minister of Finance and Economic Planning, Prof. George Benneh on the authority of the President.

The debate was commenced on July 16. The first shot at the Budget was fired by Dr. Jones Ofori-Atta on behalf of the minority parties. It was a broadside as the amendment he proposed sought to remove all the words of the Government motion apart from the staple phrase "That this House". Its terms were:

Delete all the words after "House" and insert the following words:

> "takes note of the Financial Policy of the Government for the year ending 30th June 1982 and regrets that the Financial Policy fails to deal with the fundamental and urgent economic problems of the country such as:
> the imbalance in government finances;
> the intolerable hardships faced by the ordinary Ghanaian;
> the low level of cocoa producer prices;
> the low and falling production in agriculture;
> the unacceptable high rate of inflation; and
> the loss of confidence in the cedi; and calls upon the Government to take immediate and realistic steps to tackle these pressing problems."

In seconding the amendment, Dr. G.K. Agama said that only

the previous day, the minority group had supported the passing of the Investment Code Bill. He said: "The whole country has observed the unity of purpose of this House." In other words, the minority group was opposing the Budget only because it was unsupportable. After a lengthy debate the minority amendment was supported by 54 to 51 votes. At a later date, a revised Budget presented by PNP Government was unanimously accepted.

There was also the case of the appointment of Justice Fred Apaloo as Chief Justice. There was an argument about the interpretation of the Constitution regarding the necessity for parliamentary approval. The appointment was being debated when an Opposition Member informed the Speaker that the Supreme Court had been asked to interpret the relevant Article of the Constitution. The Speaker declared the matter *sub judice* and adjourned the debate.

Dr. Hilla Limann's Government was overthrown on December 31, 1981.

A Third Preparation for the Return of Parliament

The 1992 Constitution was prepared by a 259-member Consultative Assembly under the speakership of Pe Roland Ayagitam (Chiana-Pio). For the Assembly's benefit, comprehensive proposals had been written by an appointed Committee of Experts under the chairmanship of Dr. S.K.B. Asante, some time Solicitor-General in the Busia Administration, then attached to the United Nations. Prior to the appointment of the Committee of Experts, a National Commission for Democracy had been established under the chairmanship of Justice D.F. Annan, a Member of the Provisional National Defence Council. It collected various views and embodied them in a report which was submitted to the Committee of Experts. The Constitution provided for an elected multiple-party democratic parliament consisting of not less than 140 members. The President who will be outside parliament, would appoint, with a prior approval of Parliament, his Ministers of State from among Members of Parliament, or persons qualified to be elected as Members of Parliament except that the majority of the Ministers must come from Parliament. The term of office of the President and Members of Parliament would be four years.

The draft 1992 Constitution was approved in the referendum.

For the 1992 parliamentary election, the number of seats was fixed at 2000. The presidential election was won by Flight Lt. J.J. Rawlings on the ticket of the National Democratic Congress. His running mate was K.N. Arkaah of the National Convention Party which was allied to the NDC. The parliamentary elections which were held after the presidential election were boycotted by the New Patriotic Party, the People's Heritage Party and the National Independence Party. They claimed that Flight Lt. Rawlings had won the presidential election irregularly.

The First Parliament of the Fourth Republic: January 7, 1993

Members of The Executive And Officers of Parliament

Name	Office
H.E. Flight Lt. J.J. Rawlings	President and Commander-in-Chief
H.E. Kow Nkensen Arkaah	Vice-President
Hon. Alhaji Mahama Iddrisu	Minister of Defence
Hon. J.H. Owusu-Acheampong	Minister of Parliamentary Affairs
Hon. Dr. Kwesi Botchwey	Minister of Finance
Hon. Sqdr. Ldr. C.M.K. Sowu	Minister of Works and Housing
Hon. H.R. Sawyerr	Minister of Education
Hon. Dr. Mrs. Christine Amoako-Nuamah	Minister of Environment
Hon. Mrs. Emma Mitchel	Minister of Trade and Industry
Hon. Dr. Ato Quarshie	Minister of Roads and Highways
Hon. R. Kwame Peprah	Minister of Mines and Energy
Hon. D. K. Amankwah	Minister of Lands and Forestry
Hon Dr. Obed Asamoah	Minister of Foreign Affairs
Hon. Col. E.M. Osei-Wusu	Minister of the Interior
Hon. Cdre. Stephen G. Obimpeh	Minister of Health
Hon. Ibrahim Adam	Minister of Food and Agriculture
Hon. D.S. Boateng	Minister of Employment and Social Welfare
Hon. A.K. Forson	Minister of Justice and Attorney-General
Hon. Alhaji B.A. Fuseini	Minister without Portfolio
Hon. Mrs. Vida A. Yeboah	Minister without Portfolio
Hon. Godfrey Abulu	Minister without Protfolio

Name	Office
Hon. E.K. Fosu	Minister without Portfolio
Hon. Alhaji Amidu Sulemana	Minister without Portfolio
Hon. Kwamena Ahwoi	Minister for Local Government and Rural Development
Hon. Edward Salia	Min. of Transport and Communications
Hon. Totobi Quakyi	Minister of Information
Hon. Dr. G.K. Akorsah	Minister of Science and Technology
Hon. Dr. S.A. Ayidiya	Minister of Tourism
Hon. E.T. Mensah	Minister of Youth and Sports
Hon. Lt. Col. Abdulai Ibrahim	Regional Minister, Northern
Hon. Sheriff Ahmed Gumah	Regional Minister, Upper East
Hon. J.E. Ekuban	Regional Minister, Central
Hon. I.K. Adjei-Mensah	Regional Minister, Brong-Ahafo
Hon. Dr. John F. Abu	Regional Minister, Western
Hon M.A. Gizo	Regional Minister, Greater Accra
Hon. Daniel O. Agyekum	Regional Minister, Ashanti
Hon. Paul K. Peprah	Regional Minister, Eastern
Hon. Yileh Chireh	Regional Minister, Upper West
Hon. Modestus Ahiable	Regional Minister, Volta
Victor Selormey K.B. Amissah-Arthur	Deputy Ministers, Finance
Dr. Kwabena Adjei	Deputy Minister, Lands and Forestry
Cdre. P.M.G. Griffiths	Deputy Minister, Transport and Communications
Amadu Seidu	Deputy Minister, Roads and Highways
Peter Vaughan Williams	Deputy Minister, Employment and Social Welfare
Simon Abingya Kwaku Addae-Gyamera	Deputy Ministers, Minies and Energy
Francis Korbieh	Deputy Minister, Local Government and Rural Development
Mrs. Margaret Clarke Kwesie	Deputy Minister, Health
Major Emmanuel Tetteh	Deputy Minister, Food and Agriculture
Kwabena Kyere	Deputy Minister, Education
Martin Amidu	Deputy Minister, and Deputy Attorney-General
Dan Abodakpi	Deputy Minister, Trade and Industry
Dr. Farouk Brimah	Deputy Minister, Environment

Name	Office
Dr. E.A. Ayirebi-Acquah	Deputy Minister, Youth and Sports
P.K. Owusu	Deputy Minister, Transport and Communications
Kwaku A. Bonful	Deputy Minister, Interior
Kofi Amankwah Peasah	Deputy Minister, Science and Technology
Mr. Jonathan R. Owiredu	Deputy Minister, Trade and Industry
Prof Kofi Nti	Deputy Minister, Education
Mrs Joana Appiah-Dwomoh	Deputy Regional Minister, Ashanti
Nasamu Asagibi	Deputy Regional Minister, Northern
Gilbert Seidu Iddi	Deputy Minister, Northern, Agriculture
Dan Akushie Dr. A.M. Laryea	Deputy Regional Ministers, Greater Accra
Kojo Maama Dadam George Mason	Deputy Regional Ministers, Brong-Ahafo
S.P. Adamu	Deputy Regional Minister, Western
Faisal Anaba Donal Adabre	Deputy Regional Ministers, Upper East
Victor Atsu Ahedor E.K. Aboagye	Deputy Regional Ministers, Volta
H.Q. Jehu-Appiah	Deputy Regional Minister, Central
Ampem Danquah W.B. Asante	Deputy Regional Ministers, Eastern
Bede Ziedong	Deputy Regional Minister, Upper West
Hon. J.H. Owusu Acheampong	Majority Leader
Dr. Owusu Agyekum	Minority Leader
Hon. Alhaji B.A. Fuseini	Deputy Majority Leader
Samuel Nuamah Donkor	Deputy Minority Leader
Rt. Hon. Justice Daniel Francis Annan	Speaker
Hon. Dr. Mohamed Ibn Chambas (Later replaced by) Kenneth Dzirasah	First Deputy Speaker
Hon. Dr. S.B. Arthur	Second Deputy Speaker
S.N. Darkwa	Acting Clerk of Parliament
K.E.K. Tachie	Senior Assistant Clerks
Rex Owusu-Ansah J.S.E. de Graft-Johnson	
S.O. Dodoo	Acting Editor of Debates

Party Representation: National Democratic Congress (189);

National Convention Party (8); Eagle Party (1); Independent (3). (There were 16 women).

First Sitting of the First Parliament of the Fourth Republic
This was held at the Accra International Conference Centre on January 7, 1993 with the Acting Clerk, S.N. Darkwa presiding.
After prayers, Justice Daniel Francis Annan was elected Speaker. He was conducted into the Chamber where he submitted himself to the will of the House. He took and subscribed the Oath of Allegiance and the Speaker's Oath. After being placed in the Chair, he made his speech of Acceptance. Dr. Mohammed Ibn Chambas and Dr. S.B. Arthur were elected First and Second Deputy Speakers.
Members present took and subscribed the Oath of Allegiace and the Oath of a Member of Parliament.
The House was adjourned sine die.

State Opening of the First Parliament of the Fourth Republic: April 29, 1993
After prayers the President, Flight Lt. J.J. Rawlings and the Vice-President, K.N. Arkaah were received into the Chamber.
The President delivered the Sessional Address. Its length was consistent with the total of the periods during which Ghana had been ruled without Parliament, that is to say eleven years and six days, as compared with eleven consecutive years during which Charles I reigned without the British Parliament. The President began:

> "Seventh January 1993 marked an important stage in our country's quest for a constitutional order enshrining freedom and justice. During what was known as the "lost decade" for Africa, we in Ghana revived our economy and achieved steady growth; we built reads, rehabilitated our ports and harbours, our telecommunications systems; we extended electricity to all regions of the country; we made productive activity on our farms, and in or mines and factories more rewarding. We undertook the reform of our educational system to make it more relevant. We encouraged and attracted foreign investments and sought to make our economy cope with the demands of a very com-

petitive world."

He deplored the anti-social activities which caused filth in streets and markets, unhealthy public places of convenience and bush-fires.

He said that a good number of the electorate were afraid that constitutional and parliamentary procedures could fail to reflect the urgency needed to address national problems. He referred to the constitutional provision stopping chiefs from taking part in active politics. He said that provision required clarification in the light of other constitutional provisions allowing chiefs to be appointed to public office. He continued:

> "I would also like to express my intention to establish regular interaction between the Legislature and the executive beyond the formal requirements of the Constitution.
>
> The Divestiture Programme has been an important element in our economic policy and is of special importance in the 1993 Budget... Our programme aims at providing resources in the country and also infusing capital into these enterprises through selling government shares either wholly or partially. Through divestiture we are bringing interested new investors to revitalize several enterprises which were on the verge of collapse."

President Rawlings spoke about agriculture. He said that despite some outstanding successes, there was need for greater effort. Facilities would be provided for increasing food production, and the marketing and storage of food. Ghana must maintain its distinctive position as the supplier of the finest cocoa. Tourism should be expanded but must be guarded against the negative social effects which have been experienced in some developing countries. He talked about plans formulated for improving maternity and child health services including family planning. A National Health Insurance Scheme would be introduced.

He concluded:

> "On the 7th January, all of us made the solemn pledge to observe and defend the provisions of the Constitution of

the Fourth Republic. Upholding the Constitution is also the responsibility of the entire people of the country who, through the referendum of April last year, fully endorsed it. Let us therefore together strive to make the Constitution an instrument for ensuring the peace, progress and prosperity of our country."

After the Sessional Address the President and the Vice President departed.

The House was adjourned till May 4.

Some Highlights of the First Parliament of the Fourth Republic
The striking feature of this Parliament was the absence of a virile opposition group. The largest opposition party was the New Patriotic Party which refused to participate in the 1992 parliamentary elections. Two parties represented were the National Convention Party and the Egle Party which were in alliance with the dominant NDC. Although the NDC Members did no agree with every government proposal, the cut-and-thrust of debate was not in evidence.

The legislation that sent shivers down the nation's spine was the Value Added Tax Act of 1995. One, any measure that imposes additional tax is naturally unpopular. Two, it was felt that while this kind of tax was all right in principle, the law as designed in Ghana would introduce such hardships as did not characterise the system in other countries. Three, there was also the strong suspicion that the Act was a dictate of the International Monetary Fund. The hue and cry raised about the Act made the Government suspend its operation.

The legislation that most exercised academic minds and the common sense of the people was the Constitution of the Republic of Ghana (Amendment) Act of 1996. Out of the 14 clauses of the Bill, 13 sought to change the Constitution by amendment, and one by repeal. Two subjects were of particular concern to most people: dual citizenship and participation of chiefs in active politics. Parliament agreed to the proposal to allow dual citizenship and rejected that for the participation of chiefs in active politics.

There were conservative political theorists who objected to the whole idea of amending the 1992 Constitution in 1996 on the grounds that it was too early to touch the Constitution. They also felt that a constitution should be amended abstemiously. The Government which sponsored the Bill felt that a constitution was living system created for the purpose of managing our lives; and that it must be malleable rather than rigid, that is to say subject to amendment according to necessity and absolutely regardless of time-frame.

The passage of the Criminal Code (Amendment) Act of 1995 posed questions about gender influence. By this Act the penalties for rape and defilement of a female under 14 years were increased. The women MPs pressed for even stiffer penalties, but this was resisted by their male counterparts. The incident itself may not be of great moment, but students of gender attitudes will find it significant. Should one's gender be allowed to influence one's judgement in a case like this? Should there be, for instance, a difference in attitude between a male judge and a female judge trying a case of rape?

On December 27, 1996 Kofi Annan, Secretary-General of the United Nations, visited the House.

In his Address he said his appointment as Secretary-General was not only an honour for himself but also for Ghana and Africa, both Anglophone and Francophone. He said:

> "Let me say that I expect the task to be difficult, to be complicated, to be arduous, but with the support of men and women like you, with the support of a whole nation and the prayers of our people, and with the goodwill I have around the world, there is a ground swell of goodwill and harmony which I would hope to channel into constructive development at the United Nations.
>
> The question of leadership is an interesting one, and let me leave you with a thought by Pope John Paul I, the Pope who reigned for only three months. Talking about authority and responsibility, he said it reminded him of a time when he was a bishop in a small village in Italy. He used to watch the boys play football in the courtyard, and he noticed something very interesting. When the ball was inflated, filled with air, the boys rushed and kicked it, as if they had the right to kick it; but when it was deflated and there was no air, they took no interest in it at all; and he

said this is the lot of those in authority and with responsibility. I think we all share that in this room and we have to be conscious of that.

When you get into authority, you may not change but people around you change, and if you are not careful you will also change. So I have reminded them (my close colleagues) that if they change they are going to be in trouble with me. And I have also requested them, if I change, to pinch me.

With these few words, Mr Speaker, I would want to thank all of you for the support, for the enthusiasm; and I would do my best not to let you down, or to let the world down.

Thank you very much."

The 1993/1997 Parliament broke new ground by introducing the End of Session Public Forum. At the end of every Session, parliament gave an account of its stewardship, and members of the public were allowed to ask questions. This was a new dimension of public relations which has proved quite popular and heightened general awareness of the part Parliament plays in the life of the people.

The 1993 Parliament was dissolved on January 6, 1997, having lived out its statutory four-year-life. But the claim that it was the first Parliament to do so is based on a misconception. The First Parliament of the First Republic was opened on July 2, 1960 and dissolved on May 26, 1965; so it lasted five years less 34 days, which in the parliamentary calendar is five years. The child born on July 2, 1960 would have been five on July 2, 1965. But parliamentary life is not reckoned in the same way as human life.

Polling Day in 1996 was December 7. In the weeks preceding that day, the absence of MPs from Parliament was so prevalent that a quorum was difficult to get. The incidence of absenteeism would have been worse if a greater number of them had been re-nominated by their constituencies. The 1993 Parliament was dissolved on January 6, the day before the first Sitting of 1997 Parliament. As it is, the problem of what MPs consider "inevitable absence" is bound to recur in the weeks preceding Polling Day in the year 2000. MPs will naturally campaign for their re-election. Britain acknowledges this, and the timetable of the House of Commons for 1997, a British election year is as follows:

> March 21, Breakfast for Easter Recess;
> April 8, Dissolution of Parliament;
> May 1, Polling Day;
> May 7, First Sitting of House of Commons for Election of Speaker and Swearing-in of Members;
> May 14, State Opening of Parliament.

This gives British MPs three weeks for a serious campaign.

Under the 1992 Constitution, Parliament continues for four years from the date of its first Sitting and then stands dissolved (Article 113 (1)). Clause (3) of the same Article appears to pose a conundrum. It says:

> "Where, after a dissolution of Parliament, but before the holding of a general election ... the President shall cause to be summoned the Parliament that has been dissolved to meet."

This envisages circumstances in which a general election is held after the Dissolution of Parliament which is not in consonance with Clause (1). Dissolution before general election was standard practice in Ghana before the 1992 Constitution. It is still the standard practice in Britain. It may be observed that a Parliament in session but deserted by Members for the reason that they want to ensure the survival of their own incumbency is not healthy either for the nation or for Parliament. This matter is worth the serious consideration of Parliament.

S.N. Darkwa contributed an article to the January 1997 issue of "The Parliamentarian", journal of the parliaments of the Commonwealth. In that article, which is reproduced as an Appendix, and entitled "Parliament stands undissolved while Ghana goes to the polls," Darkwa shares Ayensu's concern about MPs being absent from Parliament during the election campaign period. He raises the more fundamental issue of the possible inability of any authority in Ghana to dissolve Parliament before the end of its statutory life. What would happen if the Government after being heavily defeated on a Motion of

Confidence, resigns? Both authors are worried by the innovation of a parliamentary general election before the dissolution of the House.

The 1996 General Elections

These were held on December 7. Flight Lt. J.J. Rawlings was elected President on the ticket of the National Democratic Congress and its allies. His running make was Prof. J.E. Atta Mills, also of the National Democratic Congress.

Members of the Executive And Officers of Parliament

Name	Office
H.E. Flight Lt. Jerry John Rawlings	President and Commander-in-Chief
H.E. Prof. John Evans Atta Mills	Vice-President
Hon. Alhaji Mahama Iddirisu	Minister of Defence
Hon. Kwame Peprah	Minister of Finance
Hon. J.H. Owusu-Acheampong, M.P.	Minister of Parliamentary Affairs
Hon. Kwamena Ahwoi	Minister of Local Government
Hon. Dr. Mrs. Christine Amoako-Nuamah	Minister of Education
Hon. Dr. Mrs. Eunice Brookman-Amissah	Minister of Health
Hon. Nii Okaidja Adamafio, M.P.	Minister of the Interior
Hon. Edward K. Salia	Minister of Transport and Communications
Hon. Dr. Kwabena Adjei, M.P.	Minister of Food and Agriculture
Hon. Mrs. Vida Yeboah, M.P.	Minister of Tourism
Hon. Dr. John Abu, M.P.	Minister of Trade and Industry
Hon. E.T. Mensah, M.P.	Minister of Youth and Sports
Hon. Mohammad Mumuni, M.P.	Minister of Employment and Social Welfare
Hon. Cletus Avoka, M.P.	Minister of Lands and Forestry
Hon. Isaac Adjei-Mensah, M.P.	Minister of Works and Housing
Hon. J.E. Afful, M.P.	Minister of Environment, Science and Technology
Hon. Ekwow Spio-Garbrah	Minister of Communications
Hon. Mrs. Margaret Clarke Kwesie Awoonor	Minister of Hon. Prof. Kofi Minister of State

Name	Office
Hon. Abdullah Salifu, M.P.	Minister of State
Hon. D.S. Boateng	Minister of State
Hon. Kwabena Fosu, M.P.	Minister of State
Hon. M.A. Seidu, M.P.	Minister of State (will assist in a liaison between Executive and Legislature)
Hon. Joshua Alabi	Regional Minister, Greater Accra
Hon. D.O. Agyekum	Regional Minister, Ashanti
Hon. Kojo Yankah, M.P.	Regional Minister, Central
Hon. Alhaji Amidu Sulemana, M.P.	Regional Minister, Upper West
Hon. Donald Adabre, M.P.	Regional Minister, Upper East
Hon. Mrs. Esther Lily Nkansah	Regional Minister, Western
Hon. Gilbert Iddi	Regional Minister, Northern
Hon. David Osei-Wusu, M.P.	Regional Minister, Brong Ahafo
Hon. Miss Patience Adow	Regional Minister, Eastern
Hon. Lt. Col. C.K. Agbenaza, M.P.	Regional Minister, Volta
Hon. Nuamah Donkor	Deputy Minister of Health
Hon. Owuraku Amofa	Deputy Minister of Tourism
Hon. Victor Selormey	Deputy Minister of Finance
Hon. Mrs. Ama Benyiwa-Doe, M.P. Hon. Austin A. Gamey, M.P.	Deputy Ministers of Employment and Social Welfare
Hon. Mike Hammah, M.P. Hon. Steve S. Akorli, M.P.	Deputy Ministers of Roads and Highways
Hon. Albert Bosomtwi-Sam	Deputy Minister of the Interior
Hon. Clement Bugase, M.P. Hon. Asiedu Nketia, M.P.	Deputy Ministers of Food and Agriculture
Hon. Dan Abodakpi, M.P.	Deputy Minister of Trade and Industry
Hon. Martin Amidu	Deputy Minister of Justice and Deputy Attorney-General
Hon. Kwabena Kyere, M.P. Hon. Dr. Mohamed Ibn Chambas	Deputy Ministers of Education
Hon. Lt. Col. E.K.T. Donkor	Deputy Minister of Defence
Hon. Cdre. P.M.J Griffiths Hon. John D. Mahama, M.P	Deputy Ministers of Transport and Communications.
Hon. Richard Dornu Nartey, M.P. Hon. Moses Nayong Bilijo	Deputy Ministers of Lands and Forestry

Name	Office
Hon. Simon Abingya, M.P.	Deputy Minister of Lands and Forestry
Hon. Alhaji Amadu Seidu, M.P. Hon. Alex Akuffo	Deputy Ministers of Works and Housing
Hon. Dr. Farouk Braimah, M.P.	Deputy Minister of Environment, Science and Technology
Hon. James Victor Gbeho	Deputy Minister of Foreign Affairs
Hon. Nassamu Asabigi	Deputy Minister, Northern
Hon. S.P. Adamu, M.P.	Deputy Minister, Western
Hon. Mrs. Joana Appiah Dwomoh	Deputy Minister, Ashanti
Hon. H.Q. Jehu-Appiah	Deputy Minister, Central
Hon. Kwasi Aboagye	Deputy Minister, Volta
Hon. George Owusu, M.P.	Deputy Minister, Brong Ahafo
Hon. J.H. Owusu-Acheampong, M.P.	Majority Leader
Hon. J.H. Mensah, M.P.	Minority Leader
Hon. Alhaji M.A. Seidu, M.P.	Deputy Majority Leader
Hon. Mrs. Gladys Asmah, M.P.	Deputy Minority Leader
Hon. R. Dornu Nartey, M.P.	Majority Chief Whip
Hon. S.K. Boafo, M.P.	Minority Chief Whip
Hon. Nii Adjei-Boye Sekan, M.P.	First Deputy Majority Whip
Hon. Mrs. Comfort Owusu, M.P.	Second Deputy Majority Whip
Hon. Sheikh I.C. Quaye, M.P.	Deputy Minority Whip
Rt. Hon. Justice Daniel Francis Annan	Speaker
Hon. Kenneth Dzirasah, M.P.	First Deputy Speaker
Hon. F.W.K Blay, M.P.	Second Deputy Speaker
S.N. Darkwa	Clerk of Parliament
Kenneth Kofi Tachie J.S.E. de Graft-Johnson Rex Owusu-Ansah	Principal Assistant Clerks
S.O. Dodoo	Editor of Debates
Blay Morkeh	Marshal

The list of Ministers, Regional Ministers, Ministers of State, Deputy Ministers and Deputy Regional Ministers as at the time of concluding this Paper, is as shown above. Dr. Obed Asamoah was appointed Minister of Justice and Attorney-General on April 18, 1997.

Party Representation: National Democratic Congress (133); New Patriotic Party (61); People's Convention Party (5);

People's National Convention (1). (There were 18 women)

First Sitting of the Second Parliament of the Fourth Republic

This was held at the New Parliament House on January 7, 1997, with the Clerk, S.N. Darkwa presiding.

After prayers Justice Daniel Francis Annan was elected Speaker (for the second time). He was conducted into the Chamber where he submitted himself to the will of the House. He took and subscribed the Oath of Allegiance and the Speaker's Oath. When he was placed in the Chair he made his Speech of Acceptance. Kenneth Dzirasah and F.W.K. Blay were elected First and Second Deputy Speakers.

Members present took and subscribed the Oath of Allegiance and the Oath of a Member of Parliament.

The House was suspended, and reconvened at the Independence Square in the afternoon, with the Speaker in the Chair.

The House was attended by the President-Elect, Flight Lt. J.J. Rawlings, the Vice-President-Elect, Prof. J.E. Atta Mills, and the visiting Head of State of Nigeria, Gen. Sani Abacha.

After prayers the Speaker invited Gen. Abacha to address the House. He began by expressing gratitude to the Government for the special invitation extended to Nigeria and himself to attend the inauguration of the President-Elect. Addressing him in particular, he said:

> "Let me on behalf of the Government and the people of Nigeria convey my warm greetings and best wishes to you. (and the Government and brotherly people of Ghana) on this historic occasion of your second inauguration as President of the Republic of Ghana."

General Abacha was glad Flight Lt. Rawlings had visited Nigeria, the first foreign visit since his re-election. He paid President Rawlings tribute for the very brilliant manner in which he handled the affairs of ECOWAS during his recent two-year chairmanship of the organisation.

He emphasised the necessity for the sub-continent to consolidate, rather than rely on external element. On the occasion of the 40th anniversary of Ghana's independence, he cherished the roles played by the nation's founding fathers, and said that the legacies of their struggle and the gains of independence should not be set aside or destroyed. He wished President Rawlings a memorable term of office, and all who had travelled to Accra a safe return journey.

The President-Elect and the Vice-President-Elect took and subscribed the Oath of Allegiance and the Oath of Office.

The President then addressed the House. He first thanked Gen. Sani Abacha, President of Nigeria and Chairman of ECOWAS for his presence and his expression of solidarity in true African tradition. He also thanked and welcomed all the distinguished guests who had travelled to Accra. He conveyed the gratitude of his family and the Vice-President's family to the people for giving him and the Vice-President their mandate. He was grateful to all who since December 31, 1981 had helped to move Ghana forward. His gratitude also went to the Chairman and staff of the Electoral Commission for the high standard they set in organising the 1996 elections.

The President commended J.A. Kufour and Dr. Edward Mahama for helping to sustain the democratic process, and for the representation of their parties in Parliament. He said:

> "Let us all, no matter our differing opinions and party loyalties, work towards our common goal which is the prosperity and well-being of all Ghanaians.
>
> Mr. Speaker, in the pursuit of this goal let us put aside ethnic, religious and other aspects of our human diversity. The common purpose which unites all of us who genuinely seek the equitable development of our country, is fair"

President Rawlings talked about the people's responsibility to move forward not only Ghana but the whole of Africa. Ghana had now become a magnet attracting international credits and investments. The infrastructure of the country had been improved by the supply of potable water and electricity, and the construction of good roads. He concluded:

> "We renew our commitment to the people of this country to whom we pledge to serve with all our hearts and with all our minds. We will work as a team to carry out the mandate that you have conferred. ... It is only the people, working with Government who can create employment

opportunities, who can manage the problems of the education and health sectors and who, in short, can be our own salvation. On my part I pledge, once again, to do my duty to all our people in this country and to ensure that our administration will be responsible, and very responsive to its onerous tasks in the spirit of love and trustfulness. I thank you most sincerely. May God continue to bless this beloved nation and each and everyone of you.
Thank you very much."

The House was adjourned till January 8.

State Opening of the Second Parliament of the Fourth Republic: January 21, 1997

After prayers the President, Flight Lt. J.J. Rawlings and the Vice-President, Prof. J.E. Atta Mills were conducted into the Chamber.

The President delivered the Sessional Address. His opening words were:

"We have met today with the intention of commencing the business of the Second Parliament of the Fourth Republic, knowing very well that the eyes of the world are increasingly focused on Ghana.

With our modest success in lifting ourselves from the depths of the economic deprivation over the last decade and a half, our achievements in the building participatory democracy within a stable political environment, the peaceful and mature conduct of our December 7th elections, and the positive signs of accommodation between government and the opposition (or the minority as some of you wish to call it) following from electoral process, let me draw your attention to the fact that international eyes are very much on us, and this is also indicated by the recognition given to our wealth of human resources by the appointment of an honourable citizen of this country, Kofi Annan as the Secretary-General of the UN, not forgetting the earlier appointment of another distinguished citizen, Dr. Thómas Mensah, then our High Commissioner to South Africa, as the first President of the newly established Maritime Tribunal; all of these have turned international spotlight very much on Ghana. This is a time for great national pride for our country, but we must also be humbled by the knowledge of the responsibilities that we bear as consequence."

He talked about the Five-Year National Development Plan, a component of Ghana-Vision 2020, the District Assemblies Common Fund, urban development, and a new national sanitation policy. He observed that while gold prices were declining, oil prices were rising, reaching the highest levels since the Gulf War.

The President said that the necessary steps must be taken to stabilise the Cedi, strengthen the Export Development and Diversification Programme, and improve the impressive gains made, especially in the area of non-traditional exports. Agriculture would continue to be the backbone of the economy. The remaining bottlenecks hindering the growth of the sector would be removed. The natural environment must be maintained and sustained to prevent pollution and degradation. The projects for the introduction of thermal power had reached advanced stages. A second fishing harbour would be built at Secondi.

President Rawlings touched on sports which had now become part of the process of national development. Sports would be upgraded, no doubt under the chairmanship of Vice-President, and new national stadium complex for integrated sports constructed. He continued:

"Some amendments were made to the Constitution in 1996. It may be necessary for some more to be made to make the Constitution a living document."

He ended his address by saying:

"I would like to think that we believe and understand what we are doing here, why we are here. Let us provide the leadership, let us provide the service, let us provide the measure of integrity that the country is asking for. This is all I ask of you. May God bless you.
Thank you very much."

The President and the Vice-President departed.
The House was adjourned till the following day.

Highlights of the Second Parliament of the Fourth Republic
Although the first Sitting did not take place till January 7 1997, there have been several sparks of excitement in the proceedings.

Soon after the commencement of this Parliament, the question of the appointment of Ministers of State and Deputy Ministers began to loom large in the House. The view of the minority group was that as at January 7, 1997 appointees had, like their appointing authority himself, exhausted their mandate. The view of the majority group was that Minister and Deputy Ministers appointed upon the approval of Parliament in 1993-1997 continued to exercise their functions at the President's pleasure.

Early in February, the President's Office informed the Speaker by letter that the President had decided to retain certain named Ministers of State. The minority view on this was that "retention" of Ministers, in contrast with appointment of Ministers, was unknown to the law and the Constitution. In a bid to resolve the argument, the Minority Leader, J.H. Mensah took out a writ asking the Supreme Court to give a true and proper interpretation of certain provisions of the Constitution. Subsequently (on February 13), the Minority Leader wrote to the Speaker:

Mr. Speaker,

APPOINTMENT OF MINISTERS: ARTICLE 78 (1) OF THE CONSTITUTION

With reference to the President's letter to you of 10th February 1997 (ref.ops 807) and the various consultations that have taken place on the issue of the appointment of Ministers, I would be very grateful if you would confirm that in submitting the names listed in the first paragraph of his letter as members of his new cabinet, the President was inviting Parliament to exercise its power of prior approval of their appointment as Ministers.

I am seeking this confirmation in order to be assured that no action in Parliament is taken which in any way prejudices the determination of the constitutional issues raised in my writ of which you have notice.

I would be grateful for an urgent response to this letter.

Yours sincerely,
J.H. Mensah
Minority Leader

The Speaker responded urgently:

Hon. J.H. Mensah
Minority Leader

Dear Sir,

APPOINTMENT OF MINISTERS: ARTICLE 78 (1) OF THE CONSTITUTION

I acknowledge the receipt of your letter Ref. No. MLO/PH/0011 dated 13th February 1997 on the appointment of Ministers (Article 78 (1) of the Constitution).

My reading of the express words of the letter from the President's Office leads me to the view that all the names of the persons proposed, whether they are retained Ministers or newly nominated Ministers, were submitted to the House for the purposes of the discharge of the House's constitutional responsibilities in relation to the approval of Ministers.

Processes and procedures leading to approval or rejection of Ministers remain entirely within the competence and authority of the House. I agree that no action may be taken in Parliament which in terms of our Standing Orders prejudices the determination of the constitutional issues raised in your writ which is now pending before the Supreme Court.

Yours sincerely,

D.F. Annan
Speaker

On February 14, the House adopted the First Report of the Appointments Committee on Ministerial Nominations. In the Report, presented by the Committee's Chairman, Kenneth

Dzirasah, the Committee decided on February 13 that where an incumbent Minister or Deputy Minister is retained as a Minister or Deputy Minister by the President, it should not be necessary for him to be summoned to appear before the Appointments Committee for recommendations to be made to Parliament on his re-approval in view of the previous parliamentary approval. This decision was accepted by the House in the form of a Resolution. The minority group, having walked out of the Chamber, did not vote on the Resolution.

On 28 May, the Supreme Court ruled on the case by the minority group challenging the constitutional status of the retained Ministers in the second Parliament of the fourth republic.

The Court, by a unanimous decision, ruled that "every presidential nominee for ministerial appointment, whether retained or new, requires the prior approval of Parliament". Thus the Court upheld the contention of the minority group that by the combined effect of articles 58(1), (2) and (4), 78(1) and (2), 79(1) and (2), 80, 97(1), 100(1) and 113(1) of the 1992 constitution, the tenure of office of a Minister or Deputy Minister is conterminous with the term of the President and the Parliament. And that on expiry of the term of the President and Parliament, the tenure of the Minister or Deputy Minister also come to an end.

Accordingly, on the inauguration of a fresh term of a President and Parliament, all Ministers and Deputy Ministers nominated for office need the prior approval of that new Parliament irrespective of whether the nominee was a Minister or Deputy Minister in the previous term.

The court, however, decided by a majority of four to one that the term, "prior approval" is not a term of art. In other words, "prior approval" does not connote "consideration and vetting" and that no court can question how Parliament goes about exercising its powers of approval. On the other hand, the court held the view by a majority of four to one that "a newly inaugurated Parliament cannot immediately be ready with its various committees to approve presidential nominees".

(An article by S.N. Darkwa on the issue of parliamentary vetting of Ministers was published in the October 1997 issue of *The Parliamentarian* under the title "The constitution, and not Parliament, is supreme". It is reproduced as an Appendix).

An earlier attempt by the Minister of Finance, Kwame Peprah, to present the Government's Budget having been aborted by the objections of the minority group, he eventually on February 19, made his Motion for the approval of the Government's Financial Policy for the Year ending December 31, 1997.

The Minority Leader subsequently proposed an Amendment to the Motion. The text takes one's mind back to the Budget presented by the People's National Party government of President Limann on July 2, 1981. Dr. Jones Ofori Atta, representing the minority group, proposed an Amendment to the Government's Motion for the approval of its Financial Policy in terms similar to those of J.H. Mensah's proposal. The 1981 proposed Amendment asked the House, instead of approving, to take note of the Government's Financial Policy and to regret a number of failures on the Government's part. The Amendment was carried by the House and a revised budget was presented. In the contemporary case the proposed Amendment was defeated and the original Motion accepted.

Minister Peprah informed the House of the Government's intention to re-introduce the Value Added Tax law, to be effective in 1998.

It is amazing how, in a House aged only eight weeks, majority and minority Members, like grandmasters, played so skilfully on the parliamentary chessboard. Without the presence of the minority, the majority would at best have succeeded in playing solitaire, which is not exciting.

On February 11, the President of the World Bank, James D. Wolfensohn, visited the House as a distinguished person and addressed it. He said:

> "The Bank and Ghana have had a relationship for quite a long time. We have tried to give help; we have made financial assistance available to the extent of over $3 billion from the Bank and over $400 million from International Finance Corporation (IFC), and we hope that we have established a relationship of trust and confidence between the Bank and the people of Ghana. I came to Africa because I wanted to make prominent the fact that for me, the success or failure of the Bank is the success or failure of the African."

Wolfensohn talked about the private sector and the importance of private sector investment. He described inflation as the worst enemy of the poor. He loved the fact that Ghana had assuredly established itself as a place of leadership in the region. Ghana's work in peace-keeping, its assumption of international responsibilities, and the appointment of one of its citizens as Secretary-General of the United Nations, had given prominence to this great country.

Reflection on Opposition Boycott

The Speaker recently expressed his unhappiness with the minority group boycotting proceedings in the House. One thought on this matter was articulated by Norman Manley who at different times was Leader of the Opposition and Prime Minister of Jamaica. The mild-mannered Manley will be remembered as having lost the premiership in 1962 to the big, boisterous Bustamante (who in his campaign would ask the electorate: "Who gives you bread?", to which he would receive the reassuring reply: "Paa Busta"). Twenty-eight years ago Manley made this considered observation:

> "The boycott is obviously a revolutionary gesture born of frustration and despair of success by any conventional means. As a rule it is valuable only if it is accompanied by other and more overtly violent activities born of the same situation. By itself and in a country with organised parties and activity based on democratic procedures, it is clearly out of place. It could result in defeating its own objectives, leaving the Government serenely in power, and destroying the hopes of the followers of the opposition party."

The boycott is to be sharply distinguished from other forms of limited but extreme protest designed to highlight proper objections and to attract the maximum of public attention. After all, it is the heart and soul and essence of politics to succeed in being noticed.

Parliament, The Speaker and The Clerk

Parliament cannot function without the Speaker or the Clerk

who together constitute its kingpin.

The Office of Speaker is one of great dignity and notable antiquity. It was created in Britain where it dates back to 1265 when Simon de Montford was appointed to the Chair. There the Speaker is the first commander, the first on the protocol list of commoners (as distinct from peers). When he leaves office he is ennobled and may sit in the House of Lords. He is expected to preside over his House as the very embodiment of aloof impartiality. As soon as he is placed in the Chair, he must remove his party tag which must be seen to have been removed and to stay removed. At the social level he cuts himself off his party. The conception of aloof impartiality is a serious matter in Britain.

In other countries the Speaker may be a fierce political person who has designs on the presidency of the State. While in the Chair he reserves one eye for MPs to catch; the other is constantly trained on the presidential throne. On the other hand he may be one who maintains only marginal intercourse with his party. In either case, aloof impartiality is expected of him. The Speaker is also the representative and mouthpiece of the House, and the protector of is privileges and of the rights of minorities in the House.

He is both Speaker and Spokesman, yet the servant of Parliament. This was confirmed by William Lenthall, Speaker of the House of Commons in an incident which occurred on January 4, 1642. On that day, contrary to time-honoured tradition, Charles I burst into the Commons whose Members were regularly assembled, with the intention of arresting five of them who had ring-led the opposition to the King's constant demands for money.

He usurped the Speaker's Chair (his own Chair being the Throne in the House of Lords), and formally asked the Speaker to produce the five Members physically. The Commons intelligence service had enabled the House to spirit the five Members out of the Chamber. To answer the King, Speaker Lenthall humbly dropped to his knees and expressed "unequivocally and for all time, where the Speaker's first duty lay".

This is what he said:
"May it please your Majesty, I have neither eyes to see nor tongue to speak in this place, but as the House is pleased

to direct me, whose servant I am here; and I humbly beg Your Majesty's pardon that I cannot give any other answer than this to what your Majesty is pleased to demand of me."

These words established Parliament independence of the Executive, which every Speaker is bound by his most sacred duty to acknowledge, uphold and defend without counting the cost.

Although the Office of Speaker does not demand rare qualities but rather common qualities to a rare degree, the following is a high-profile expression of the Speaker's overall qualifications:

> Dignity and authority tempered with urbanity and kindness; firmness to control the persuasiveness to counsel; promptitude of decision and justness of judgement; tact, patience and firmness; and natural superiority combined with inbred courtesy so as to give, by his own bearing, an example and model to those over whom he presides; an impartial mind; a tolerant temper; and reconciling disposition; accessibility to all in public and private as a kind and prudent counsellor.

At Westminster when the Speaker is elected, a moving ceremony follows. He goes to the Bar of the House of Lords where, before the Lords Commissioners, and Lord Chancellor (the "Speaker" of the House of Lords) approves his appointment on behalf of the Sovereign. The Speaker then proceeds:

> "My Lords, I submit myself with all humility and gratitude to Her Majesty's gracious commands. It is now my duty, my Lords, in the name and on behalf of the Commons of the United Kingdom, to lay claim by humble petition to Her Majesty to all their ancient and undoubted rights and privileges, especially to freedom of speech in debate, to freedom from arrest, and to free access to Her Majesty whenever occasion shall require, and that the most favourable construction shall be put upon all their proceedings. With regard to myself I humbly pray that if in the discharge of my duties I shall inadvertently fall into any

error, the blame may be imputed to myself alone, and not to Her Majesty's faithful Commons."

One of the Speaker's main duties is to give a ruling. A ruling is the judgement he gives when he notices an infringement of a rule of the House, or when a Member rises on a point of order and complains that a rule of the House has been breached. Many, many times the Speaker has to rule that the point of order purported to have been raised is no point of order at all. MPs desirous of interrupting speech are prone to rise and say: "Mr. Speaker, On a point of order".

The Clerk is the chief advisor to the Speaker on parliamentary practice. He is available to all MPs, public officers and the parliamentary press. In the discharge of his responsibilities he must be a purist in interpreting the law. He must not countenance any form of adulteration by suffering the whims and caprices of a particular party or person to influence his judgement. If in the line of duty he incurs the displeasure, or even the wrath of anyone, he must consider it an occupational hazard. It must be observed that parliamentary practice is not some mysterious or abstruse science but just a general meeting, a company board meeting or a church synod, the conduct of proceedings is based on parliamentary practice. Knowledge of it is useful to everybody.

The Clerk arranges the Sittings of the House. He is Head of the Parliamentary Service and Parliament's accounting officer. He is appointed to office with great expectations of him, but no one appears to have particularised the ethic of his Office. The Clerk's position can be quite unenviable. The First Sitting of a new Parliament after a general election is presided over by him. Unlike the Speaker he cannot *viva voce* call a Member to speak. He must of necessity act as in a pantomime, using his hand to recognise the Member who desires to nominate a person for the Office of Speaker. If there is only one candidate, his tongue loosens after the nomination as been seconded. If the office is contested, he finds his tongue again after the secret ballot.

Comparatively, miming is fun. The Clerk's real problem begins when Members have settled in, interacted with him and assessed him in the light of their peculiar criteria. Party 'A' may feel he is pro Party 'B'. That feeling may be triggered off by a wrong vibration or by something as trivial as having an occasional noggin with a Party 'B' Member, or by something as grave as the Clerk's amorous incursion into a Party 'B' Member's home. If the incursion escalates into an invasion it can only help to strengthen that feeling.

Woe betide the Clerk if the Speaker, consulting him openly in the Chamber, give a ruling against a Party 'A' Member; the more so if the Speaker, to protect the Clerk, consults him in the Speaker's office in the presence of a Deputy Speaker belonging to Party 'A' who leaks the ruling to Members even before it is typed. Ironically, a slap on both cheeks makes the Clerk "impregnable", indeed "inconceivable" (in the sense that neither side knows the object of his supposed favours). A double slap induces nonchalance and lend him a glorious feeling of security.

During the decade or so commencing in 1954 there was always a clamour for admission cards to the State Opening of Parliament. That fever is still with the country and is strongest in supporters of the ruling party. In the Old Parliament House the wives of Ministers of State were allocated conspicuous seats in the front row of the West Gallery, the one facing the Speaker's Chair. Now and then the card for a Minister's wife got into the hands of another lady under the Minister's personal divestiture programme. The lady who for the grand occasion was invariably dressed up to the nines, was easily spotted occupying rarefied seat. Backbench MPs following the wrong scent would gang up on the Clerk and accuse him of unduly exalting some lowly maiden from his own privy chamber.

During the First Republic, Ayensu's heart skipped a beat whenever Kwame Nkrumah telephoned him at home late in the afternoon. Ayensu was not surprised by Nkrumah's question: "Ayensu, what is the matter again?" He knew instinctively that the CPP Parliamentary Sanhedrin had besought Nkrumah to sack him. He would go to Flagstaff House and explain his position, thankfully *ex-parte* to Nkrumah who would smile and say; "Sack you, and who is going to get me another Clerk?" This made Ayensu feel vindicated and ten feet tall.

No Clerk of Parliament in Ghana has ever joined a political party. It is not written law: Clerks just do not do it. In 1955, before Ayensu was promoted to the position of Clerk of Parliament, he resisted pressure from well-meaning friends in the CPP to get a CPP party card in order to dispel unfortunate rumour gaining ground. He explained that if he took a CPP party card and there was a change of government, he would by the same token have to take the new ruling party's card, and that would amount to prostituting office. Nkrumah, on getting word of this, sent for Ayensu and in the President's office in the Ministry of the Interior building, commended him on the neutral position he had taken. Nkrumah gave Ayensu a little lecture on politics and his parting words were: "Don't join any party, not even the CPP"

If the media seek the opinion of the Clerk on a controversial ruling given by the Speaker, he should not say anything. Even a retired Clerk may not wish to make a comment. Such a ruling was given by the Speaker of the House of Commons in 1979, and the just retired Clerk, contacted by the BBC, expressed disagreement with the Speaker.

In Ghana a retired Clerk may still suffer political prejudice. After the 1979 parliamentary elections, at the request of the People's National Party which had gained power, Ayensu gave a talk to its MPs. Two days afterwards, at the instance of the Popular Front Party, he repeated the talk for the benefit of its MPs. When the PNP heard about this, their copious gratitude evaporated and Ayensu was called names. Helping the opposition with knowledge was, incredibly, read as subverting the PNP cause.

A final observation: However torrid the climate, Clerks have to perform their duties without fear or favour. If in the fell clutch of difficult circumstances they should so wilt as to take the line of least resistance, this particular class of public officer will fast become an endangered species, much to the detriment of the parliamentary democracy the country has so cheerfully embraced and lovingly nurtured.

From the Clerk's Diary: Parliamentary English

Of the strange words and phrases uttered by MPs, two stand out in one's mind. The first is "nicodemusly" used as an adverb by Joe Appiah. The Bible tells us Nicodemus was the big Pharisee guy who consulted Jesus by night and in the Jewish Council. Appiah used the word to mean "very secretly," The second is "houhoudious". The word is not found in any dictionary, standard or slang. Nor can its origin be traced in any of the indigenous languages. But in those days it became popular as some of the modern words in "BBC English".

Ghana is Forty Years, but What Does the Future Hold?

Neither the oracle at any shrine nor the crystal ball will say anything about the future of Ghana. So pray:

> that our multiple-party democracy may never succumb to one-party rule or rule by decree;
>
> that every Chief Executive may ever bear in mind that to reign sovereign in the hearts and affections of the people is far more gratifying to a generous and benevolent mind than to rule over their lives and fortunes, and that to enable him enjoy that pre-eminence with honour to himself and satisfaction to the nation, he must subject his own passions and prejudices to the high dominion of charity (or love) in its most ample and beautific sense;
>
> the Speaker may walk along that lien of unerring and impartial justice laid down for his pursuit by the ancient traditions of the Chair;
>
> that the institution of Parliament may be granted permanence, progress and productivity;
>
> that its Members, clothed in humility and committed to the national cause, may pursue their labour with patience, fortitude, integrity, selflessness and zeal;
>
> that they may realise that the virtues of probity, accountability and transparency are essential for satisfying such mortals as are responsible for checking our work on earth, namely parents, employers, auditors, assessors, judges, etc.;
>
> that upon attaining that realisation they may proceed to pay due reverence to the primal virtue of truth which, enveloping all virtues and having a unique place in our hearts, is within the exclusive discernment of the one and

Only True God; that by the faithful discharge of their national mandate, our representatives may ensure that the people of Ghana, typified by the common man, or the man who rides on the no-name village hackney-bus, enjoy the quintessence of the national heritage of freedom and justice;

that our nation may be endued with Pax Ghana just as Pax Romana redounded to the joy of Roman empire for two centuries; and finally

that Ghana may be vouchsafed perpetuity lest, like its grand original, it should grow into a proud and mighty empire only to founder and sink into oblivion.

Intercession
Until the Golden Jubilee of Independence on March 6, 2007,
May He, who alone can do immeasurably more than we dare ask or desire or dream, enfold us all securely in His arms! So be it.

THE THIRD PARLIAMENT OF THE FOURTH REPUBLIC

The 2000 Elections – Consolidation Of Multi Party Democracy

The peaceful elections of 7th and 28th December 2000 reinforced Ghana's passionate commitment to multi-party democracy which we freely chose in a referendum to adopt the 1992 Fourth Republican Constitution. The elections were significant. They marked a steady progress towards the consolidation of democratic governance in Ghana.

The prospect of a smooth transfer of political power from a democratically elected government to another has eluded Ghana since Independence in 1957. The achievement of orderly political succession and peaceful transfer of power demonstrated our maturity and cohesion as a nation. For the first time in four decades, Ghana was able to hold three successive multi-party elections and the first peaceful change of government within the same Fourth Republic in 1992, 1996 and 2000.

The resilience and patience of the Opposition (the in-coming government) that had waited for almost 30 years before gaining political power and the outgoing government's concession of defeat in the elections have emphasized our determination to use the ballot box as a means of changing government.

The presidential election of 7th December 2000 was inconclusive as none of the candidates obtained the required number of votes. The New Patriotic Party (NPP) Presidential candidate, Mr. John Agyekum Kufuor and the National Democratic Congress Presidential candidate, Prof. John Evans Atta-Mills had to face a run-off on 28th December 2000.

Mr. John Agyekum Kufuor was elected the President of Ghana in the run-off. The other parties opposed to the NDC threw their weight behind the NPP.

The Third Parliament of the Fourth Republic January 7, 2001

Members of the Executive and Officers of Parliament

Name	Office
H.E. John Agyekum Kufuor	President and Commander-In-Chief
H.E. Alhaji Aliu Mahama	Vice-President
Hon. Jake O. Obetsebi Lamptey	Chief of Staff and Minister for Presidential Affairs
Hon. J. H. Mensah	Minister of Parliamentary Affairs/Government Business and Chairman of National Development Commission (he was later designated Senior Minister and Chairman of Government Economic Team.)
Hon. Dr. Kwame Addo-Kufuor	Minister of Defence.
Hon. Yaw Osafo-Maafo	Minister of Finance.
Hon. Hackman Owusu-Agyemang	Minister of Foreign Affairs.
Hon. Nana Addo Dankwa Akufo-Addo	Attorney-General and Minister of Justice.
Hon. Alhaji Malik Yakubu Al-Hassan	Minister of the Interior
Hon. Dr. Kofi Konadu Appraku	Minister of Trade and Industry.
Hon. Major Courage Quarshigah (Rtd)	Minister of Food and Agriculture
Hon. Kwadwo Baah-Wiredu	Minister of Local Government and Rural Development.
Hon. Mrs. Gladys Asmah	Minister of Women's Affairs.
Hon. Prof. Dominic Kwaku Fobih	Minister of Environment, Science and Technology.
Hon. Prof. Christopher Ameyaw Akumfi	Minister of Education
Hon. Ms. Christine Churcher	Minister of State at Ministry of Education (PrimarySecondary and Girl Child)
Hon. Dr. Richard Winfred Anane	Minister of Health.
Hon. Kwadwo Adjei-Darko	Minister of Roads and Highways.
Hon. Felix K. Owusu-Agyepong	Minister of Transport and Communications.
Hon. Dr. Kwaku Afriyie	Minister of Lands, Forestry and Mines.
Hon. Mrs. Cecilia Bannerman	Minister of Manpower Development and Employment.

Name	Office
Hon. Albert Kan Dapaah	Minister of Energy.
Hon. Kwamena Bartels	Minister of Works and Housing.
Hon. Mallam Ali Yussif Issah	Minister of Youth and Sports.
Hon. Mrs. Hawa Yakubu	Minister of Tourism.
Hon. Dr. Kwesi Nduom	Minister of Economic Planning and Regional Cooperation.
Hon. Ishmeal Ashitey	Minister of State, Agriculture (Fisheries).
Hon. Charles Omar Nyanor	Minister of State Presidency, Private Sector Development.
Hon. Elizabeth Akua Ohene	Minister of State, Advisor on Public Affairs.
Hon. Sampson Kwaku Boafo	Regional Minister, Ashanti.
Hon. Ernest Akobuor Debrah	Regional Minister, Brong Ahafo.
Hon. Isaac Eduasar Edumadze	Regional Minister, Central.
Hon. Dr. Francis Osafo Mensah	Regional Minister, Eastern.
Hon. Sheikh Ibrahim Codjoe Quaye	Regional Minister, Greater Accra.
Hon. Ben Salifu	Regional Minister, Northern.
Hon. Salifu Mahami	Regional Minister, Upper East.
Hon. Mogtari Sahanun	Regional Minister, Upper West.
Hon. Kwesi Owusu Yeboah	Regional Minister, Volta.
Hon. Joseph Boahen Aidoo	Regional Minister, Western.
Hon. Edward Osei Kwaku Hon. Alhaji Moctar Bamba	Deputy Ministers, Presidential Affairs
Hon. Edward Akita	Deputy Minister, Defence
Hon. Mrs. Grace Coleman Hon. Dr. Adombilla Agomila	Deputy Ministers, Finance
Hon. Alhaji Mustapha Ali Iddris	Deputy Minister, Foreign Affairs.
Hon. Capt. Nkrabeah Effa-Dartey(Rtd)	Deputy Minister, Attorney-General & Justice
Hon. Yaw Barimah	Deputy Minister, Interior
Hon Akwasi Osei Agyei Hon. Boniface Abubakar Saddique	Deputy Ministers, Trade and Industry.
Hon. Dr. D.K. Antwi Hon. Dr. Abel-Majeed Haroun	Deputy Ministers, Agriculture
Hon. Ms. Alima Mahama	Deputy Minister, Local Government & Rural Development.
Hon. Mrs. Anna Nyamekye	Deputy Minister, Environment, Science and Technology.

Name	Office
Hon. Rashid Bawa	Deputy Minister, Education.
Hon. Moses Baah	Deputy Minister, Health.
Hon. Seidu Alex Sofo	Deputy Minister, Roads and Highways.
Hon. Agyeman Manu Hon. Sefuni Achuliwor	Deputy Ministers, Transport and Communications.
Hon. Benjamin Osei Kufuor Hon. Clement Eledi	Deputy Ministers, Lands and Forestry and Mines
Hon. Joe Donkor Hon. John Jebbah	Deputy Ministers, Manpower Development & Employment
Hon. K.T. Hammond	Deputy Minister, Energy.
Hon. Ms. Theresa Tagoe	Deputy Minister, Works and Housing
Hon. Joe Aggrey	Deputy Minister, Youth and Sports.
Hon. Nana Akomea	Deputy Minister, Tourism
Hon. Adjei Duffuor	Deputy Regional Minister, Brong Ahafo
Hon. Narh Dometey	Deputy Regional Minister, Eastern.
Hon. Isaah Ketekewu	Deputy Regional Minister, Northern
Hon. Kofi Djamase	Deputy Regional Minister, Volta
Hon. Sophia Honer-Sam	Deputy Regional Minister, Western
Rt. Hon. Peter Ala Adjetey	Speaker
Hon. F.W.A. Blay	First Deputy Speaker
Hon. Kenneth Dzirasah	Second Deputy Speaker
Hon. J.H. Mensah	Majority Leader
Hon. A.S.K. Bagbin	Minority Leader
Hon. Paapa Owusu-Ankomah	Deputy Majority Leader
Hon. I.K. Adjei-Mensah	Deputy Minority Leader
Hon. A.O. Aidooh	Majority Chief Whip
Hon. E.K. Doe Adjaho	Minority Chief whip
Hon. Osei Kyei-Mensah Bonsu	First Deputy Majority Chief Whip.
Hon. Mrs. Gifty Eugenia Kusi	Second Deputy Majority Chief Whip.
Hon. John Tia	First Deputy Minority Chief Whip
Hon. Mrs. Comfort Owusu	Second Deputy Minority Chief whip.
Rex Owusu-Ansah	Clerk to Parliament
K.E.K. Tachie	Deputy Clerk

Name	Office
Daniel A. Ametepeh Amy Olga Forson (Ms.)	Principal Assistant Clerks
John G.K. Agama	Editor of Debates
Col. A.L. Lamptey (Rtd)	Marshal

Party Representation:
New Patriotic Party (100)
National Democratic Congress (92)
People's National Convention (3)
Convention People's Party (1)
Independent (4)
(There are 19 women including one seat won in a by-election)

In 6 by-elections held after the general elections the NPP won all the seats including 3 from the NDC.

First Sitting of the Third Parliament of the Fourth Republic

This was held at the Parliament House on January 7, 2001 with the Clerk, Rex Owusu-Ansah presiding.

After prayers, Peter Ala Adjetey was elected Speaker.

He was conducted into the Chamber where he submitted himself to the will of the House. He took and subscribed the Oath of Allegiance and the Speaker's Oath. When he was placed in the Chair he made his Speech of Acceptance.

Members present took and subscribed the Oath of Allegiance and the Oath of a Member of Parliament.

F.W.A. Blay and Kenneth Dzirasah were elected First and Second Deputy Speakers.

The House was suspended and reconvened at the open court of the Parliament House.

The House was attended by the President – elect, Mr. J.A. Kufuor, the Vice President-elect, Alhaji Aliu Mahama and the visiting Heads of State, President Abdoulaye Wade of Senegal, President Laurent Gbagbo of Cote d'Ivoire,

President Blaise Compaore of Bukina Faso, President Gnassingbe Eyadema of Togo, President Alpha Omar Konare of Mali, President Olusegun Obasanjo of Nigeria and Vice President Jacob Zuma of South Africa.

The President-elect and Vice-President-elect took and subscribed the Oath of Allegiance and the Oath of Office.

After this ceremony, the House moved to the Independence Square for the President's Inaugural Address. It may be noted that this Parliament set aside the practice of its predecessor which held the swearing-in ceremony of the President-elect at the Independence Square. The Minority side (now the majority side) in the second Parliament had argued that the Oath-taking ceremony of the President-elect "must take place in Parliament and before Parliament". They explained that the premises of Parliament include all the precincts of the House.

The President addressed the nation. He first thanked the Almighty God for the new democratic transition. He said that by the smooth transfer of power from a democratically elected government to another for the first time in our 43 years of Independence, we have demonstrated our maturity and cohesion as a nation. He said the joyous memories of this achievement would remain for a long time. He stressed that the spontaneous joy and feeling of goodwill should not be allowed to disappear without translating it to tangible improvement in the lives of the people.

President Kufuor emphasized that our greatest enemy is poverty and the battle against it must start with reconciling our people and forging ahead in unity. He said: "We have gone through turbulent times and we should not in any way downplay or brush aside the wrongs that have been suffered. I do not ask that we forget, indeed we dare not forget but I do plead that we try to forgive".

He expressed gratitude to our foreign friends for their help and encouragement and acknowledged their role in the electoral process and the deepening of democracy.

He said that his government would create an enabling environment for investment, encourage entrepreneurs so that business would flourish. He pledged to create wealth through the private sector which must be the engine of growth of the national economy. He said: "My resolution is to launch a golden age of business and enterprise in our country that would transform the lives of our people within the next decade".

President Kufuor underlined the need for sacrifice and hard work in order to be freed from poverty, hunger and disease. He pledged his administration's determination to cut waste and corruption from public life. He said: "There will be under this administration, ZERO TOLERANCE for corruption and I make a solemn pledge to you my compatriots and fellow citizens that I shall set a personal example".

President Kufuor emphasized that multi-party democracy had come to stay in our country and that there would be room for differences of opinion, both the government and political opponents have their honoured roles to play and urged all to exercise tolerance, an essential quality for deepening our democracy.

President Kufuor stated that Ghana could not build a vibrant and prosperous nation unless there was peace with our neighbors. He pledged that Ghana would play her part in helping to maintain peace in the sub-region which had been in turmoil for years.

He thanked the visiting Presidents for their presence and solidarity.

The House was adjourned till January 9, 2001.

First Message To Parliament On The State of the Nation February 15, 2001

After Prayers the President, J.A. Kufuor and the Vice-President, Alhaji Aliu Mahama were received into the Chamber.

The President delivered the State of the Nation Address. He said, inter alia:

"Last December, that is on the 7th and 28th December 2000, the good people of this country made a decision. They chose, after 43 years of national independence, to use the ballot box to effect a change of government and to replace one democratically elected government with another. The world stands in admiration of our achievement and this should encourage us in our path of deepening and consolidating democracy under a regime of respect for human rights and the rule of law"

He talked about the depth and extent of Ghana's financial plight. The performance of the economy was generally far from satisfactory at the time his government assumed power. The growth of real gross domestic growth in the year 2000 was 3.7 per cent which was lower than the budgetary target of five per cent in the previous budget statement. The total debt stock stood at 41.1 trillion Cedis out of which 31.7 trillion Cedis or US $5.8 billion was external and 9.4 trillion Cedis or US $1.7 billion was domestic. He stated that the legacy his government inherited on the economic front was daunting.

The President talked about the "Positive Change", a new vision which was eloquently articulated by the late Dr. J.B. Danquah, an eminent Ghanaian and the founder of the political tradition to which the President and his party belong. He quoted: "Our party's policy is to liberate the energies of the people for the growth of a property-owning democracy with right to life and freedom and justice as the principles to which the government and laws should be dedicated in order specifically to enrich life, property and liberty of each and every citizen" He said that his government believed in the private sector which must be the engine of growth of the national economy.

The President stressed that his government would reinforce the institution of the Presidency, support the independence and effectiveness of the judiciary and enlarge the capacity of Parliament to deliver good governance. He added that the rule of law must be the guiding principle to which every person should submit.

He underlined his commitment to reconcile our people in order to be able to tackle the many problems we face. In this connection he promised that a National Reconciliation Commission would be established in fulfillment of his party's manifesto. He said, "The National Reconciliation Committee, promised in our manifesto, will be established to provide a forum where those who are aggrieved can have the opportunity to air their grievances in order to promote the goal of national reconciliation"

The President talked about the devastation being caused by HIV/AIDS, the abolition of the "Cash and Carry" system and the establishment of national insurance scheme and his government's intention to repeal the Criminal Libel Law in order to expand the boundaries of freedom and as a mark of confidence in a responsible media.

He concluded: "I urge all well-meaning Ghanaians to join us in moving towards the realization of our common dream of peace, progress and prosperity".

"May God help us all"

Parliament and the Media
Parliamentary reporting of proceedings by the media has been

essential to the success of our multi-party democracy. Our vibrant media has played a vital role as the main link of communication between parliament and the people from the First Parliament to the Third Parliament of the Fourth Republic.

As the watchdog of the people's interests especially in the absence of the Opposition in the First Parliament, the media kept on informing the public of what was happening in Parliament and exposing weaknesses in the administration and ensured that the government was accountable to the electorate.

Parliament and the media need each other. Members of Parliament would seek media coverage and the media would look for news that will sell their newspaper. But the media must not pander to the politicians. Rather, the media must exercise its responsibility to expose and criticize fairly and objectively. Whenever fair and objective criticism gives way to sensation – seeking the media and Parliament are likely to enter into an adversarial relationship. Parliament and the media cannot do without each other. They must be seen as an ally, each complementing and supplementing the other in safeguarding the public interests.

The media should not misrepresent or ignore Members even if they do not say what the media want them to say. Nor should Members be ignored even if they are slow and hesitant in speech or boring. The media must have a sense of balance in the coverage of the proceedings in Parliament and give each Member a fair coverage.

As Members enjoy certain privileges the media must ensure that the reputations of Members are not destroyed by manufacturing news instead of undertaking the hard work of honest investigation. While Members whose reputations are injured by fabricated stories may invoke parliamentary privilege to impose punitive sanctions, Parliament must be less sensitive to criticisms made in good faith and use their privileges sparingly. Fair and objective media coverage of Parliament is a pre-requisite to establishing friendly relationship between the media and Parliament. The media have performed well to inform the public of what goes on in Parliament. The House has generally exercised restraint on imposing sanctions on breaches of its privileges.

Some Highlights of the Third Parliament of the Fourth Republic
Openness is one of the strengths of multi-party democracy. It

allows free and frank public discussion of matters of national importance. The value of media friendly relations and open government was not lost on the NPP government. President Kufuor took an early step to open up his administration to the media whose adversarial relationship with former President Rawlings was seen as one of the major factors that contributed to the electoral defeat of the NDC government in the 2000 elections.

In acknowledgment of the media vital role in multi-party democratic development, the President allowed the media unrestricted access to the Castle, the seat of government. The NPP administration also discontinued the ongoing prosecutions against some journalists for criminal or seditious libel.

The passage of the Criminal (Repeal of Criminal Libel and Seditious Laws) (Amendment) Bill was in fulfillment of the government's commitment to the process of deepening and consolidating multi-party democracy in the country.

The repeal of these laws, used in the colonial and recent times to harass and browbeat the media, has provided an environment conducive to enhance freedom of expression characterized by open discussion in the radio and the media. The repeal of the laws must also be seen as a mark of confidence in a responsible media.

The legislation that won the hearts and minds of most Ghanaians was the National Reconciliation Commission Act of 2002. The legislative process provided a forum for public participation and input into the Bill that helped to improve the quality of the legislation. Although there was overwhelming national support for the legislation, its passage was by no means easy. To the credit of Members, Parliament did not ram the Bill through the House. The Bill was introduced in the House on July 20th, 2001 and was subjected to close scrutiny for several months before it was passed. The debates that followed were sometimes marked by controversy, heat and provocation and a walkout by the Minority side.

The people's desire for such a piece of sensible legislation was not lost on the House. When all was said and done, good sense prevailed and rigid preconceived positions gave way to consensus in the public interest and democracy. Thus the fruitful exercise of national reconciliation began with Members themselves.

The main object of the Bill was to establish an accurate, complete historical record of human rights violations and abuses inflicted on persons by public authorities dating from independence to the beginning of the Fourth Republic and recommendations made to the President for appropriate redress to promote national reconciliation.

The National Reconciliation Commission held its first public hearings on January 14, 2003.

The Centre for Democratic Development (CDD), a non-governmental organisation played a vital role in organising a public forum for both international and local participation in the formulation of the policy for national reconciliation.

PART TWO:

DEVELOPMENT OF THE PARLIAMENTARY SYSTEM IN GHANA UNDER THE FOUR REPUBLICS

Legislative authority in Ghana has been vested in Parliament which has exercised it in varying degrees under the four constitutions the country has had since independence in 1957. Having closely watched the operation of Parliament under the four republics, the authors find it necessary to examine, even if briefly, each of the four constitutions, particularising how parliament has performed under it and drawing lesson for the benefit of the country.

The 1957 Independence Constitution

The Transitional Constitution of 1954 provided for the direct election of 104 Members of Legislative Assembly on the basis of universal adult suffrage. As far as the legislature was concerned, the difference between the Transitional Constitution of 1954 and the Independence Constitution of 1957 lay not so much in detailed provisions as the character of the Assembly.

The former constitution gave the country an advanced colonial legislature and at independence the country attained a sovereign parliament. The 1957 Constitution introduced a parliamentary system a-la- Westminster under which the Prime Minister and all Ministers of State were Members of Parliament elected on party lines. An important feature of this constitution was an attempt to decentralise the administration of the country by the creation of Regional Assemblies.

The 1960 Republican Constitution

This Constitution introduced an Executive President and a Parliament consisting of the President and the National Assembly. A distinction was made between Parliament and National Assembly. The word Parliament was used both generally and specifically. In its generic sense it described a legislative body; in its specific sense it described an institution comprising the President and that legislative body.

For an Act of Parliament to be effected, it required the passing of a Bill by the National Assembly and the subsequent Assent of the President to that Bill. Both components of Parliament, the President and National Assembly, had a part to play in bringing a law into effect.

This Constitution (and its subsequent amendment in 1964) conferred special legislative powers on the first President during his initial period of office. The Legislation he might wish to make would take the form of directions given by a Legislative Instrument whenever he considered that the national interest demanded it. It must be pointed out that such a Legislative Instrument could not affect the Constitution or repeal any other enactment; it could only alter such enactment.

The President appointed his Ministers from among Members of Parliament who introduced bills in the House. The President, in obedience to the Constitution, attended Parliament in person to deliver a Sessional Address in which he gave a report on the state of Ghana.

Castigation of Parliament Under the First Republic
In February 1964 the Constitution was amended to entrench a one-party system of government. The 1969, 1979 and 1992 Constitutions were careful to deprive Parliament of the power to pass legislation to effect a one-party-state.

A number of criticisms have been levelled against the First and Second Parliaments of the First Republic. The opinion was much canvassed that the 1964 amendment was not only inglorious but that it also subdued Parliament to an appreciable degree. For fear of being branded dissident, Members usually fell in line with executive wishes. Debates were often preceded by unsolicited adulation of the President. The few who found courage to give utterance to their conscience, as in 1961, 1965 and 1966, either fled the country or were detained or unseated in Parliament.

The celebrated confrontation between Parliament and the Executive after the heated debate on the 1964 Budget Statement, had the effect of reducing Parliament virtually to a rubber stamp. Too many Bills were hastily passed upon Certificates of Urgency, and the absence of parliamentary committee system deprived the House of the opportunity to scrutinise legislative proposals in depth. The power to enact retrospective legislation was so abused that the 1969, 1979 and 1992 Constitutions restricted Parliament's power to pass such legislation. Other major weaknesses were the confrontational style of politics and the lack of consensus on national issues.

But Parliament had its strong points. It had a clear vision of what it wanted and pursued it vigorously. It was firm and forthright, and indecision was not one of its drawbacks. If the excessive powers conferred on the first President are taken away, the authors find the constitutional arrangement of the Executive President and the Legislature forming the two components of Parliament, a more tempting proposition.

The 1969 Constitution

The 1969 Constitution made substantial provisions to reduce undue concentration of power in any one organ of the State. It emphasised the need to ensure that the three arms of Government, i.e. the Executive, the Legislature and the Judiciary were independent of one another, that is to say no one of them should be in a position to control the State. The system of government chosen under the 1969 Constitution was a parliamentary one. In this system it was necessary for Parliament to trust the Executive and accept the legislative programme of the Cabinet, while maintaining its right to amend Bills, question executive actions and defeat the Government as a last choice. The Cabinet was under the leadership of a Prime Minister who was *primus inter pares* in a body to which the administration of the nation was entrusted.

In the parliamentary or cabinet system of government, there was a titular or ceremonial Head of State. In reality, the powers of government were vested in the legislative body. The Cabinet was collectively responsible as a Government to the legislative body of which they were also members. If the policies of Cabinet were rejected, the Government was expected to resign. The alternative was for the Government to seek a Dissolution of Parliament in order to appeal to the people for another mandate to be given to it in a general election.

The ceremonial President in the Second Republic was vested with powers to summon, prorogue and dissolve the National Assembly. He had the power to refuse to assent to a Bill passed by the National Assembly, to make appointments to important offices of State, as well as the prerogative of mercy.

The President appointed the Prime Minister who had to be a Member of Parliament. The Prime Minister and his Cabinet formed the Executive. The Prime Minister appointed Ministers from among Members of Parliament and decided which of them should serve on the Cabinet.

Legislation was initiated by the Cabinet and presented by Ministers to the National Assembly, but Private Members also had power to promote legislation. The Minister also were all Members of Parliament and open to questioning by Members about any matter falling within the portfolio of their respective Ministries.

It may be remarked that Parliament under the 1969 Constitution attracted many high-calibre persons. This was mainly because candidates for the general election knew that there was a good chance of their being appointed to ministerial office. They could not get these positions if they were not on both sides of the House and the legislative programme was impressive. The Constitution reinforced the parliamentary committee system under which expert advice was sought and Bills scrutinised before their presentation for debate. The committee system also helped to enhance debate and public participation in the legislative process, that increased public awareness of the work of Parliament.

This Constitution was based on a multiple-party system, the leader of the party with the highest number of seats in the Assembly being asked to form a government.

The view has been expressed that the restriction of ministerial office to Members of the Assembly possibly deprived the Prime Minister of the opportunity to appoint to the Cabinet many capable persons who did not want to be involved in the hustle and bustle of general election. As all Ministers were appointed from within Parliament, the Prime Minister could not appoint a Cabinet Minister from one region (Volta) where he lost his potential ministers in the general election. The constitution-makers of 1969 felt that any person who wanted a ministerial position should face the electorate.

The 1969 Constitution prescribed a Parliament whose legislative powers were limited and were subject to the provisions of the Constitution – the supreme law of the nation. A provision was made that "any acts of the Legislature which were found to be inconsistent with any provisions of the Constitution shall be to the extent of that inconsistency void and of no effect". This provision was repeated in the 1979 and 1992 Constitutions, and power was given to any person to seek redress in the courts if he felt that there was an infringement of any provision of the

Constitution. More importantly, the Constitution also restricted Parliament's power to enact legislation to turn Ghana into a one-party state.

The 1979 Constitution

The 1979 Constitution provided for a presidential system of government on the American pattern, but maintained the single-chamber Legislature. The President was the Chief Executive and had considerable powers conferred on him. Ministers were chosen from outside Parliament in conformity with the principle of the separation of powers between the Executive and the Legislature.

The Legislature was weakened by the absence of Ministers in the House. If a Minister was chosen from Parliament, he ceased to be a Member, thereby depriving the Legislature of some of its able Members. The position was made worse for Parliament when a number of its experienced and able Members were appointed Ministers.

What is more, Ministers were not subject to the same degree of accountability to Parliament as in 1969. Question Time, the most lively feature of parliamentary proceedings, when the Prime Minister and his colleagues were subjected to searching questions, was belatedly introduced – in 1981.

Again, Private Members were not well equipped to initiate legislative proposals. In fact, with the exception of one or two Bills by Private Members, all the Bills were initiated by the Executive. Because the new House was not conversant with parliamentary procedures and practices, Parliament took too much time to settle into serious business.

Some interesting features of this Parliament may be mentioned. Despite the initial difficulties, the Parliament of the Third Republic achieved some success. It asserted its independence of the Executive and had the singular distinction of being the only Parliament to reject the Budget presented by a Government with a majority in Parliament. It also began determining national issues by consensus, rather than party strength.

With regard to the 1979 Constitution, it has been observed that the American Executive President, in spite of his many powers, is held in check by a powerful Congress and a Judiciary with a long tradition of independence from the Executive. Apart from these constitutional curbs on the U.S. President's powers, there are various pressure groups whose views and feelings he cannot lightly ignore. The federal nature of the American Constitution also places a limitation on the powers of the President.

In the absence of the above-mentioned constraints, an American-style presidency can easily become excessively authoritarian. On the other hand, a weak President may pander to the wishes of a virile and hostile Parliament. Both the 1969 and 1979 Constitutions were adopted after an extensive testing of opinion and the consideration of various alternatives. The term of the National Assembly was five years in the Second Republic, and in the Third Republic as well.

The 1992 Constitution

Ghana, whose Parliament was in abeyance for over a decade, returned to constitutional rule on January 7, 1993. The previous elected Government had been overthrown by the military on December 31, 1981. In 1992, a 259-member Consultative Assembly prepared a new constitution. The Draft 1992 Constitution was approved by the people in a referendum. The 1969 and 1979 Constitutions had been promulgated by Constituent Assemblies.

The 1992 Constitution was approved by an overwhelming majority. It provided for an elected multi-party democratic parliament consisting of not less than one hundred and forty Members. The 1969 and 1979 Constitutions of the Second and Third Republics had provided for 140 elected Members. For the 1992 parliamentary elections, the memberships of Parliament was increased to 200. The old Parliament House could not accommodate the 200 Members; so Parliament temporarily moved to the International Conference Centre. Parliament has now moved its new House, popularly called Kwame Nkrumah Conference Centre, which is within the State House Complex. Before then the building underwent massive rehabilitation and renovation.

The term of office of Members of Parliament is four years. The First Parliament of the Fourth Republic consisted of three parties, namely the National Democratic Congress (189 seats), the National Convention Party (8 seats) and the Egle Party (1 seat). Sixteen women were included among the 200 members, and 2 women among the 3 independent members.

The main opposition parties – the New Patriotic Party, the People's National Convention, the Peoples Heritage Party and the National Independence Party – were conspicuous by their absence from the First Parliament of the Fourth Republic. They boycotted the 1992 parliamentary elections. However, three opposition parties participated in the elections of the Second Parliament. A late election was held in the Afigya Sekyere East Constituency which was won by the NPP bringing opposition seats in Parliament to 67. The ruling party – the National Democratic Congress (NDC) – won 133 seats in a Progressive Alliance with the Eagle party (EP) and the Democratic People's Party (DPP) which did not support any candidates of their own. The main opposition parties in the Great Alliance consisted of the New Patriotic Party (NPP) (61 seats), the People's Convention Party (PCP) (5 seats) and the People's National Convention (PNC) (1 seat). The number of women members increased from 16 in 1992 to 18 in 1996.

Since devolution of power has been central to the democratic process initiated by the Provisional National Defence Council, regional bodies had to be created to deal with matters affecting each region as a whole. The districts have also benefited from decentralisation of power through District Assemblies created under the Constitution.

Some Comparisons Between the Four Republics

The First Parliament of the First Republic (1960-1965) and the First Parliament of the Fourth Republic (1993-1997) completed their statutory terms of office. The life of the Independence Parliament of 1957 was cut short by the nation's desire to become a republic. The Second Parliament of the First Republic and the Parliaments of the Second and Third Republics had their terms terminated by military intervention.

The First Parliament of the Fourth Republic was dissolved on January 6, 1997 and the Second Parliament inaugurated the next day. The Constitution provides that the President may serve two terms. The main features common to all the four parliamentary constitutions since independence were as follows:

    The Speaker's Office, Deputy Speaker's Office;
    The Clerk's Office;
    Government and Opposition Parties in Parliament –

except for the period of the one-party system (July 1965 to February 1966) which ended with the fall of the First Republic;
Regulation of proceedings in Parliament by Standing Orders; and
The Committee System.

Under the First Republican Constitution, the Executive President was not a Member of Parliament but Ministers of State had to be appointed from among MPs, and they had to sit in Parliament to pilot Bills and deal with other matters that fell within their portfolios.

The President, in obedience to the Constitution, attended Parliament to open it formally and deliver the Sessional Address in which he reviewed the state of the Nation. Under the Independence Constitution and the Constitution of the Second Republic, the Prime Minister and all Ministries of State appointed by him had to be MPs. The President had the function of placing the final seal on Acts of Parliament to give them legal power. The Third Republican Constitution was based on the American Presidential System with strict separation of power between the executive and the legislature.

Under the Fourth Republican Constitution, based mainly on the American system of government – a blend of the Parliamentary and presidential systems in which the Executive President appoints a majority of his Ministers from within Parliament and the others from outside Parliament with the prior approval of Parliament. The latter category of Ministers can participate in debate in the House but have no vote.

A HYBRID OF WESTMINSTER AND CONGRESS SYSTEM OF GOVERNMENT IN GHANA[1]

What are its Strengths and Weaknesses
At Independence in 1957 Ghana adopted the Westminster model of parliamentary democracy. We practiced this system of government almost flawlessly from 1957 to 1960 in the first Republic

---

1. This article was first published in the Third Issue of the *Parliamentarian*, a journal for Commonwealth Parliaments in September 2004.

and 1969 to 1972 in the second Republic. Parliaments in both Republics were vibrant and produced some political giants whose debating skills and incisive wits enlivened debates. Both sides were determined to pursue their parliamentary business with seriousness of purpose. They exploited the procedural opportunities available to both the government and the opposition with lively debates. The government was forced to declare and defend its policies and justify its actions while the opposition opposed the policies and the reasons for their dissent and offered alternative programmes. There were quick thinking MPs whose oratory held the House spellbound and who always had an attentive audience packing the public galleries.

There were, however, a few drawbacks in the first republic. The absence of strong committee system did not help the legislative process that must involve public participation and input into the making of the law. Public participation in the formulation of public policy and Bills is essential because the laws we make affect every citizen whose input into the legislation may improve its quality. Again the incidence of Bills passed upon certificate of urgency was high which denied the public any avenue for direct participation in the legislative process. A result of this was that a many Bills were rammed through Parliament to the detriment of the public.

Another drawback for the Parliaments of the first republic was the confrontational style of politics with government and opposition holding rigid preconceived positions, which never gave way to consensus even on vital national issues. When Ghana adopted one party state from 1965 to 1966 there was little enthusiasm for the existence of that Parliament. A great deal of powers was conferred on the first President.

The 1969 constitution of the second republic provided fundamental changes in the previous constitutions. Ghana restored the multiparty Westminster parliamentary system and a strong committee system was established, with standing and select committees to which every Member belonged. Avenues were open to the public for their direct participation in the formulation of public policy and Bills. The legislative programme was impressive and the high caliber persons on both sides of the House enriched debates. Speaker Justice Ollenu was prompted to remark that it would take a generation to have another Parliament like the one under the Second Republic.

Some weaknesses in the previous Constitutions

After experimenting with both the Westminster form and the presidential system with a reasonable measure of success, what was the purpose of adopting a combination of the two different systems of government? The Parliaments of the three republics, like any human organizations, were beset with a few problems or weaknesses.

The imposition of the one party state where 198 Members were returned unopposed in parliamentary election in 1965 provided an immediate pretext for a coup that cut short the life of that Parliament.

Although the 1969 Constitution corrected some of the weaknesses in the constitutions before it, such as concentration of power in the executive, and lack of effective committee system, an enfeebled Parliament and a high incidence of passage of Bills upon certificate of urgency, the Westminster Parliamentary system also created an ethnically unbalanced cabinet. The constitution required that Ministers were appointed from among Members of Parliament. The ruling Party led by Prime Minister, Dr. K.A. Busia lost his potential Ministers in the Volta Region. The exclusion from cabinet of the second largest ethnic group in Ghana was disturbing.

The Third Republican constitution of 1979 was based on the American system with strict separation of powers between the Executive and the Legislature. Ministers did not belong to the Legislature but the President appointed several able Members as Ministers thus depriving Parliament of some of their best legislators. As a result, the minority side, containing several Members who had parliamentary experience in the second republic, exploited procedural devices to defeat government budget for the first time in Ghana's Parliament and also intelligently used procedural opportunity (sub judice convention) to abort debate and ruling on a motion for appointment of the Chief Justice nominated by the President. The defeat of the government budget could have brought the government down in a parliamentary system. It was not so under the 1979 constitution, and in the 1992 constitution neither. Few observers have attributed the budget defeat to the ineptitude of the leadership of the majority side. The budget was defeated by 54 votes against 53.

Central purpose of the hybrid system

The constitution framers of 1992 were clearly influenced by factors such as political instability that could give a pretext to those who would seek to impose their will on others through coercion or armed rebellion.

We can say that the central purpose of this hybrid system of government is designed to ensure that the executive and Parliament are working along the same lines. Through constraints on both Parliament and its committees the system does not encourage rivalry between the executive and Parliament that may be seen or construed by others as a source of political instability.

Some of the factors that constrain Parliament and its committees in their oversight of the Executive are:

- Although the legislative power in Ghana is vested in Parliament the bulk of the legislation is initiated by the executive. It is a daunting task for a private Member to initiate a Bill in Parliament. It requires funding, drafting and research assistance, which are not easily available. And above all, it requires winning the support of the majority side. Private Member's bill has not been patronised in our Parliament. Available record indicates that only one such was introduced by J.A. Kufuor in the third Republic.
- Parliament does not vote (appropriate) money unless the executive proposes it; nor does the House impose or increase taxes unless the executive requires such taxation in accordance with Article 108 of the constitution.
- The bulk of the time is taken up in government business.

These constraints especially article 108 which gives financial initiative to the executive, and Article 78 of the constitution which requires that the President shall appoint majority of his Ministers from among Members of Parliament, have attracted much public criticism. Professors Kwasi Prempeh and Mike Ocquaye, a constitutional lawyer and a political scientist respectively, have argued strongly that these constraints have enfeebled Parliament in its oversight responsibilities over the executive. In their view Article 108 must be amended to enable Parliament to offer and sponsor alternative legislative solutions to public problems.

They also contend that the power of the President to appoint majority of MPs as Ministers undermines Parliament's oversight function. Members who become Ministers and those who aspire to become Ministers would not feel inclined to be critical of the executive. Theoretically, this is a respectable argument. But functionally, it is difficult for MPs to abandon the party on whose ticket they entered into Parliament. This is not to say that both sides should always hold rigid preconceived positions that would not give way to consensus on vital national issues.

In any of the three systems, Westminster and Congress as well as the hybrid, if the government have majority in Parliament, the power of Parliament becomes the power of government. Majority was voted to Parliament because the Members belonged to a party with a Manifesto that was approved by the electorate to implement. As long as each party maintains Whips, Backbenchers have limited scope for independent action if they want to retain their seats in the next election. If free votes are regularly allowed, a government may have lower figure of support for than whipped votes. Even though article 113(1) of the constitution would not allow dissolution of Parliament as a result of defeat for the government's budget or of a lost vote of confidence, regular lower majority votes for the government would be regarded as a loss of face, and possible defeat in the next election.

Advantage of Ministers' presence in Parliament
The constitution requires that the elected Ministers and non elected Ministers can participate in the proceedings of Parliament, but the latter cannot vote in the House; nor can their presence form part of the quorum.

The presence of Ministers in Parliament has distinct advantages. Unlike in the past, the responsibilities of modern governments and legislatures have increased in volume and have become complex. They have to grapple with not only the conduct of foreign affairs, defence, promotion of trade and administration of justice, but also with health, education, industry, sciences and matters relating to the economy. When it comes to these complex and technical issues, the executive has access to civil servants, experts and can hire consultants. Ministers in possession of information in concise and comprehensible form enlighten and enrich debates in the House.

On the other hand, our MPs lacking technical and adequate support staff, research assistants and well equipped library cannot expect to make meaningful contributions to debate.

When we practiced the American presidential system, which excluded Ministers from Parliament, in the third republic the adversarial relationship between the executive and Parliament was in evidence. The two were usually set on a confrontational course. Question time was more like an inquisition: a Minister was actually told "to go and sin no more" after being subjected to rigorous questioning.

As Dr. S.K.B. Asante, at one time a Solicitor-General of Ghana and Chairman of the Committee of Experts on Constitutional Proposals for the 1992 constitution, put it: "Ministers who had no connection with Parliament (in the third republic) showed little inclination to appear before it; or render any accounting to it in respect of their executive performance". In fact, the then Attorney-General, Joe Reindorf initially opposed the appearance in Parliament of Ministers to answer parliamentary questions in the presidential system. This Parliament sensibly began to adopt consensus style of politics because the government had a majority of two, one of whom was incapacitated through illness.

Dr. Asante further noted that apart from the third Republic (1979 to 1981) all constitutional arrangements of Ghana since Independence have made provision for the appointment of Ministers from Parliament. It is generally agreed that membership of Ministers in Parliament engenders a feeling of togetherness and "allows MPs some leverage over Ministers who are more deferential to the authority of Parliament than Ministers appointed from without".

Indeed, co-operation between the executive and Parliament generally brings better results. The question that has exercised the minds of constitutional and political observers is: will the separation of the executive from Parliament necessarily end partisan politics in Parliament?

A government that achieves political power in a multiparty democracy must expect the support of MPs in the same party. The defiance of party Whips would mean that the declared will of the electorate and the government's programme cannot be implemented, although a defeat of government on any major issue cannot bring it down as per article 113(1) of the constitution.

It is, however, suggested that on a matter of deeply held personal conviction, a dissident may be allowed to vote against a decision of the party at his or her own risk.

The Whips in the United States Congress may not apply their discipline on the Members without taking into consideration local, district, regional or state issues which were the basis of their election. Representatives are elected bi-annually and their local or regional issues may not necessarily coincide with the national issues. As it has been observed "in the US oversight has become an expression of rivalry between two powerful bodies (the executive and Congress) each of whom is unmovable until the next elections."[2]

Against the backdrop of our past experiences, the constitution framers of 1992 felt that co-operation between the executive and Parliament would generally bring better results but not necessarily result in the executive dominance over the Legislature. No one should soon expect ideological or partisan ceasefire in the hybrid system. Confrontation over issues would occur in the Chamber and minority will have its say but the Majority may have its way.

Although constrained by limited resources and time the House and its committees can exercise effective scrutiny of government on particular subjects that the government would prefer the Committee and the House to leave alone. The Public Accounts Committee, for example, can interrogate Ministers and Senior Civil and Public Officers in a way that the House itself cannot do through the use of question time. Parliament and its committees, adequately resourced with technical support staff, a well equipped library, research assistants and adequate funding to hire experts, can exercise effective oversight responsibilities over the Executive.

THE COMMITTEE SYSTEM
The development of Committees
A feature common to the Second, Third and Fourth Republican Parliaments is the Committee System. The Constitutions on which it was based required that various Parliamentary Committees should be appointed to enquire into the activities and administration of such Ministries and Departments as fall within their terms of reference. A very important function of the Committees is to examine in detail Bills that are referred to them and, after making such enquires as they consider expedient, propose such amendments as are necessary.

---

2. Parliamernt and Congress: Kenneth Bradshaw and David Pring: p.355

Owing to the volume of legislative work and its complexity, it is felt that if legislators are going to carry out their assignments thoroughly, they need a certain amount of specialised knowledge. It is also recognised that the House as a whole can hardly work with despatch and efficiency on Bills or other forms of legislation, the scrutiny of financial measures and the oversight of the Executive which are the main functions of Parliament.

The Committee System ensures efficient despatch of the business of Parliament. Under this system the House is divided into a number of Committees covering all major fields. It has been observed that it is in a Committee that a Member does his real work.

Committees of Parliament of the First Republic

The Committees of Parliament of the First Republic were classified into Sessional Select Committees and Ad Hoc Committees. The Sessional Select Committees were appointed at the beginning of each Session for the duration of that Session. They could only make recommendations for adoption by the House, but when so empowered by the House they could take a decision. Ad Hoc Committees were appointed as and when the need arose.

There were five Sessional Select Committees: the House Committee, the Committee of Privileges, the Public Accounts Committee, the Business Committee and the Standing Orders Committee.

House Committee

The duties of the House Committee include advising the Speaker on all matters connected with the comfort and convenience of Members.

Committee of Privileges

The Committee of Privileges is responsible for enquiring into complaints of contempt of Parliament and matters of privilege referred to it.

Public Accounts Committee

The Public Accounts Committee has the duty of examining the public accounts showing the appropriation of the sums granted by Parliament to meet public expenditure, and such other accounts as are laid before it, together with the Auditor-General's reports on the accounts. The Committee is required to submit its report to the House at least twice in a Session. The Committee is usually chaired by a senior Opposition Member. The Committee, backed by the Auditor-General, has a high reputation as a financial watchdog.

Business Committee
The Business Committee determines the business of each Sitting and the order in which it is to be taken.

Standing Orders Committee
The Standing Orders Committee considers proposals submitted from time to time for the amendment of the Standing Orders.
It must be noted that there were no specific Committees to examine Bills during the First Republic.

The Committee System after the First Republic
The 1969 Constitution gave prominence to the Committee System. Having carefully considered the legislative process of the First Republic, during which a large number of Bills were passed upon Certificates of Urgency, the constitution framers of 1969, 1979 and 1992 decided that the Legislature should hasten slowly in making laws. The public were sometimes unaware of the Bills passed upon Certificates of Urgency. The constitution makers recognised that the legislative process was of educational value for the people, and therefore must be given wide publicity. The public must also be made to participate in the process as fully as is consistent with sound parliamentary practice. The Constitutions of 1969, 1979 and 1992 made it compulsory for any Bill introduced in the House for the First Reading to be referred to the appropriate Committee. The report of the Committee with an explanatory memorandum would form the basis of debate and eventual passage of Bill, with or without amendment, or its rejection.

Committees of Parliament of the Fourth Republic
The Standing Orders of Parliament of the Fourth Republic prescribe two main types of committees the Standing Committees and the Select Committees. In addition to these, the House may appoint Ad Hoc Committees.

The Sessional Select Committees under the First Republic have now become Standing Committees in the parliaments of the Fourth Republic. The 8 Standing Committees are:
  The Standing Orders Committee,
  The Business Committee,
  The Committee of Privileges,
  The Public Accounts Committee,
  The Subsidiary Legislation Committee,
  The Finance Committee,
  The Appointments Committee, and
  The Committee of Members Holding Offices of Profit.

Following an amendment to the Standing Orders which came into force on November 30, 1995, the Committee on Government Assurances was added to the Standing Committees.

Comparisons between Standing Committees of the House of Commons and the Ghana Parliament

In the Commons, Standing Committees are primarily designed to examine Bills through debate. They are given the task of taking the Committee Stage of Bills in a formal, predetermined manner and they deal with Bills only. In Ghana both Standing Committees and Select Committees may have Bills referred to them, although it is rare to have a bill referred to the former except the Finance Committee.

One notable characteristic of the Standing Committees of the House of Commons is their impersonality. They are distinguished from each other alphabetically. They are called Standing Committee 'A', Standing Committee 'B', and so on. In Ghana's case, Standing Committees are called by their functions, e.g. Finance Committee and the Public Accounts Committee.

Standing Committees do not (except in extreme circumstances) defeat a Bill in the Commons. They can amend a Bill, and sometimes drastically, but when the Bill goes back to the House, the House may reverse the Committee's recommendations. In short, the Committee's task is to improve a Bill rather than defeat it.

Membership of Committees Reflects Party Strengths in the House

Members of both Standing Committees and Select Committees are nominated by the Committee of Selection whose Chairman is the Speaker. The Committee of Selection has to ensure that party strengths in the Committees reflect those in the House as a whole in accordance with the provisions of the Constitution. This has two implications. First, it would mean that Members belonging to small parties and the independent members may not qualify for a place on the Committees in which they are interested. Second, when party strengths in the House are fairly equal, the majority's strength in a Standing or Select Committee should only be minimal, that is, not sufficient to prevent Bills from being amended in a manner unacceptable to the Ministers.

Chairmen of Committees

A peculiar nature of Standing Committees in Ghana's Parliament is that of seven out of the eight have their Chairmen prescribed by the Standing Orders. These are the Business Committee, Committee of Privileges, House Committee, Public Accounts Committee, Appointments Committee, Standing Orders Committee and Committee on Members Holding Offices of Profit. The revised Standing Orders which came into force on November 30, 1995 have given powers to the Committee of Selection to appoint Chairmen and Vice-Chairmen of Committees.

Size of Committees

The size of a Standing Committee is also fixed by a standing order: it should be 29 or 30 to ensure that the composition of the Committee will as much as possible reflect the different shades of opinion in Parliament in accordance with Article 103 of the Constitution.

As has been pointed out earlier, the constitutional provision that party strengths in the Committees should reflect those in the House as a whole, has two implications. One, Members belonging to small parties and independent Members may not qualify for a place on the Committees in which they are interested. Two, when party strengths in the House are fairly equal, the majority's strength in a Committee should not be sufficient to prevent Bills from being amended in a manner disagreeable to Ministers.

Non-Partisan Approach to Work in the Public Accounts Committee

The hallmarks of the Public Accounts Committee are its non-partisan approach, its detailed examination of matters, and its ability to advise the House on the best course of proceeding with any matter. It is heartening to know that the reports of the Public Accounts Committee are usually above party politics. This Committee has invariably managed to achieve a high degree of unanimity in its findings and recommendations.

Select Committees

Parliament's Standing Orders provide for 16 Select Committees such as the Committee on Food, Agriculture and Cocoa Affairs, and the Committee on Health and Education. They are known as departmentally-related Committees because they are concerned with the expenditure, administration and policy of Departments of Government. While it is rare for a Bill to be referred to a Select Committee in the House of Commons, almost all Bills presented in Ghana's Parliament are referred to the appropriate Select Committee. Select Committees in Ghana's Parliament also have an investigatory function, and their proposals may lead to legislation.

Meetings of Committees

Ghana's Parliamentary Committees are largely masters of their own proceedings: they decide how to set about their given tasks and they can do this in any way they think fit, provided that they work within their prescribed terms of reference. They may meet weekly, or more frequently if there is urgent work. Meetings are sometimes open to the public, but when Members deliberate among themselves, over their report, they always do so in private.

Committee of the Whole House

The Committee of the Whole House is now rarely used in our Parliament. This Committee used to meet in the Chamber of the House in the course of a Sitting of the House, and one could hardly distinguish between proceedings in the full House and those in a Committee of the Whole House. In the Committee of the Whole House the Speaker's Chair is empty, the Committee being chaired by a Deputy Speaker or a temporary chairman who takes the Clerk's seat at the Table of the House. The Mace is tilted instead of resting erect. The rules of debate are relaxed, members being allowed to speak more than once on any question. The Committee is exclusively concerned with legislation. Both Ghana and Australia have proposed to abolish this Committee because there is no rational basis for the exclusion of the Speaker during its meeting in the Chamber. When the Commons introduced this Committee, the Speaker who was then appointed by the King, was suspected of being his agent. This is no longer the case.

Powers of Committees
Parliaments are usually reluctant to allow their Committees too much scope or power: they must operate in the shadow of the House that created them. But in our case the Constitution give them many powers for their efficient operation. The power to send for persons, papers and records is conferred on Committees by the Constitution (Article 103) and the Standing Orders. If a person summoned to appear before a Committee refuses or fails to attend, his conduct may be reported to the House as a contempt and he may be ordered to attend at the Bar of the House. If he does not obey this order, he may be ordered to attend at the Bar of the House. If he does not obey this order, he may be ordered to be sent for in the custody of the Marshal of the House. Members of the House including Ministers, are invited but not summoned to meetings of a Committee. The power to send for persons, papers and records enables a Committee to carry out investigations, hear witnesses, assemble facts, and generally conduct the enquiry. Witnesses can be examined on oath, and perjury can attract statutory penalties. In their interest witnesses are protected by the privileges of the House, in respect of evidence they give from such consequences as slander. The power to send for papers and records is rather limited; it is confined to such departmental documents as are not of an internal kind: in other words departmental files and minutes cannot involving national security. Faced with an official refusal to disclose information, a Committee's only redress is to report this to the House where the refusal may be supported if the Government has a majority there.

When appropriate, Committees are given powers to adjourn from place to place, allowing them to travel in order to see things for themselves. They also have powers to set up Sub-Committees, seek the assistance of expert advisors, and sit when the House is to recess.

Some Committees are deliberately excluded from discussing policies of the Government as a natural consequence of their function. The Public Accounts Committee, for instance exists to examine departmental accounts, and these are matters connected with administration. However, because of the character of their work they could look equally at policy and administration. Committees are given the power to report. A report concludes the Committee's proceedings. Committees have a certain amount of influence but little power. Power actually remains in the House, and Committees remain the House's creatures. Witnesses, official or otherwise, may however be asked to produce memoranda on the matters in question. These, coupled with the information that may be extracted by cross-examination, are enough to ensure that most Committees get the information they want.

Advantages of the Committee System

The functions of Committees include the scrutiny of legislation, the scrutiny of financial measures, and the oversight of the Executive. The effectiveness of parliament may therefore be measured by the quality of the work of its Committees in these and other areas. One of the several merits of the parliamentary committee system is the opportunity for dialogue between legislators and the public. It is not possible for the public to participate in debates in the Chamber. But the public may be permitted to present memoranda to, and be heard by a Committee. Such public hearings have an educational value for both parliament and the public. The Committees also enable the Legislature to scrutinise the activities of he Executive most effectively in the area of legislation.

Business in the Chamber has always been dictated by the need to get certain laws passed while at the same time allowing a number of other parliamentary processes to take place. As a result, the House is often hard-pressed to find time on its floor to examine a matter of national importance when it arises. If a

Select Committee is given terms of reference to deal with the matter in question, it can find sufficient time to delve deep into it. In this way the time of the House is not encroached upon.

Another merit of the Committee System is that it enables Members to gain experience in dealing with a subject, and so be able to exert influence which they would not otherwise have. In this way they specialise in certain fields. Again, work done in Committees, especially in the Public Accounts Committee, is less partisan than that done on the floor of the House.

The Committees seek to reduce the areas of administration that the Government may wish to keep secret. In this way, Committees hold the Government to account, even if imperfectly. It may be observed that even in cases where Committees divide strongly, much information is nevertheless revealed which would otherwise remain secret. These advantages can be aded to the usefulness of Committees in saving time on the floor of the House, and doing work for which the House, sitting as a whole, is unsuited.

At a recent meeting of the Clerks of Commonwealth Parliaments, a member put forward a proposal that Committees of Parliament should be given more powers to do their work as in the case of the United States Congress. The argument against this position is that a strong Committee system in Parliament may enable small groups of Members to take decisions which are contrary to the wishes of the House as a whole; give some Members a better opportunity to exert power and influence than others; and turn their chairmen into tin gods. The present Committee System in Parliament is not likely to be subject to these defects.

The Fourth Parliament of the Fourth Republic January 7, 2005

At the time of going to press, Ghana had successfully held another Parliamentary and presidential elections on 7th December 2004 one month before the end of the tenure of the legislature and the Presidency of Mr. J.A. Kufuor.

Unlike the 2000 inconclusive presidential election, president J.A. Kufuor was able to reach the threshold of more than fifty percent (50%) of the votes for victory to secure his second term. The largest opposition NDC party candidate, Prof. J.E. Atta Mills ran second. The President won over 52. percent while Prof. J. E. Atta Mills had over 44. percent of the votes.

In the Parliamentary elections the ruling New Patriotic Party (NPP) obtained 128 seats, National Democratic Congress (NDC) 94 seats, People's National Congress (PNC) 4 seats, Convention People's Party (CPP) 3 and Independent 1.

The representation of women in Parliament increased from 19 to 25 seats

The House elected its new Speaker, Ebenezer Begyina Sakyi-Hughes on 7th January 2005 to become the ninth Speaker since Independence in 1957.

Members of the Executive

Name	Office
H. E. Mr. John Agyekum Kufuor	President and Commander in Chief
H. E. Alhaji Aliu Mahama	Vice President
Mr. J.H. Mensah	Senior Minister
Mr. Kwadwo Baah-Wiredu	Minister for Finance and Economic Planning
Mr. Yaw Osafo-Maafo	Minister for Education and Sports
Dr. Kwame Addo Kufuor	Minister for Defence
Mr. Ayikoi Otoo	Attorney General
Maj. Courage Quarshigah(Rtd)	Minister for Health
Prof. Mike Oquaye	Minister for Energy
Papa Owusu-Ankomah	Minister for the Interior
Nana Addo Dankwa Akufo-Addo	Minister for Foreign Affairs
Mr. Charles Bentim	Minister for Local Government and Rural Development

Name	Office
Prof. Dominic K. Fobih	Minister for Lands, Forestry and Mines
Mr. Ernest K. Debrah	Minister for Food and Agriculture
Mrs. Gladys Asmah	Minister for Fisheries
Hajia Alima Mahama	Minister for Women and Children's Affairs
Mr. Hackman Owusu Agyeman	Minister for Works and Housing
Mr. Alan Kyeremanteng	Minister for Trade & Industry
Mr. Dan Botwe	Minister for Information
Mr. Jake Obetsebi-Lamptey	Minister for Tourism & Modernization of the Capital City
Mr. Albert Kan-Dapaah	Minister for Communications
Mr. F.K. Owusu-Adjapong	Minister for Parliamentary Affairs
Mr. Kwamena Bartels	Minister for Private Sector Development & Presidential Special Initiatives
Prof. Christopher Ameyaw Akumfi	Minister for Harbours and Railways
Mr. Joseph Kofi Adda	Minister for Manpower, Youth and Employment
Mr. Yaw Barimah	Regional Minister, Eastern
Mr. S.K. Boafo	Regional Minister, Ashanti
Mr. Joseph Boahen Aidoo	Regional Minister, Western
Mr. Boniface Gambila	Regional Minister, Upper East
Mr. Ambrose Dery	Regional Minister, Upper West
Mr. Kofi Dzamesi	Regional Minister, Volta
Nana Sienti	Regional Minister, Brong Ahafo
Mr. Boniface Saddique	Regional Minister, Northern

APPENDICES

TRIBUTE TO THE LATE K.B. AYENSU
By S.N. Darkwa (co-author)

K.B. Ayensu, co-author of this book, died on June 17, 1997 at the age of 76 years. He was the first Clerk of Parliament in independent Ghana, having been promoted to that position in 1955 at the age of 34 years. He was also the longest serving Clerk and served under the distinguished Speaker, Sir Emmanuel Quist for whom "K.B." had unbounded admiration.

"K.B." made immense contributions to the growth and development of Parliament in Ghana. He established Parliament's work culture and standards, and drew up its Standing Orders. Blessed with a clear mind and an enormous capacity for work, he put in place procedures and practices that, though modelled after Westminster, were nevertheless tailored to our own particular circumstances. Under him, an almost flawless parliamentary machine was created to serve the National Assembly. Among his notable contributions to the development of Parliament was his 1965 publication, *Parliamentary Practice and Procedures* which shed immense light on the technical and difficult field of parliamentary business. He engineered the inclusion of Ghana's Parliament in the Commonwealth Parliamentary Association headquartered in London. He also manoeuvred for the Parliament of the First Republic to be admitted to the Geneva-based Inter-Parliamentary Union.

Indeed, the fact that Ghana's parliamentary procedures and practices, as well as the basic machinery for servicing Parliament, have survived the military interventions of the past three decades, bears testimony to the enduring legacy that K.B. Ayensu bequeathed.

CONSTITUTIONAL PRACTICE
Parliament stands undissolved while Ghana goes to the polls

Mr. Sam N. Darkwa, in Accra
An election was called for one month before the existing Parliament could be dissolved constitutionally, leaving Members torn between the campaign and the Chamber.

Parliamentary elections are usually preceded by the dissolution of Parliament. Under this practice, Parliament may run its full term of office or cut short its life through dissolution before elections are held for the next Parliament.

The power to dissolve Parliament at any time may be vested in the Prime Minister or the Head of State. Parliament can be dissolved earlier (through prorogation) before its full term or automatically by efflux of time. At the dissolution, the life of the House comes to an end. It has often been said that dissolution "passes a sponge over the parliamentary slate" and all matters pending before it or any of its committees are quashed.

Following a Different Practice

The practice of dissolving Parliament before an election has much to commend it. In the Ghanaian situation, however, the country went into parliamentary and presidential elections while Parliament remained undissolved. Ghana held elections on 7 December 1996, while the life of Parliament was to continue until 6 January 1997 since the first Parliament of the fourth republic was inaugurated on 7 January 1993 for four years.

Few could foresee the consequences of this situation when the Electoral Commission fixed the date for the election, without the dissolution of Parliament, in compliance with the provisions of the 1992 constitution. Article 113 (1) of the constitution provides a constitutional limit to the term of parliament: "Parliament shall continue for four years from the date of its first sitting and shall then stand dissolved."

This means that no person or authority other than the constitution can terminate the life of Parliament before it has completed its full term. Neither the unpopularity of the policies of the government nor a vote of no-confidence would be sufficient grounds for dissolution of Parliament for a fresh election.

A Remedy for Past Maladies

The situation where Ghana held an election before dissolution may be explained against the backdrop of our experiences. For the 40 years of independence, two out of the four Parliaments did not survive their full term of office. The life of the Parliament of the second republic lasted for only 27 months, while the Parliament of the third republic also came to an abrupt end after 27 months through military interventions.

In search of constitutional and political stability, the constitution-makers felt that no person or authority other than the constitution should have the power to end the life of a parliament before it has completed its full term of four years "except that when Ghana is engaged in war Parliament may from time to time, by resolution supported by not less than two-thirds of all the Members of Parliament, extend the period of four years for not more than 12 months at a time". This provision was also intended to constrain any government that would want to perpetuate the life of parliament without an election. Parliament is supreme in law-making; but the 1992 constitution imposed considerable limitations on the legislative powers of Parliament. Its capacity to make laws is so restricted it is not omnipotent. For example, Parliament cannot pass a law to make Ghana a one-party state. Any law passed by Parliament which is inconsistent with any provision in the constitution may be challenged by any citizen of Ghana and may be declared by the Supreme Court to be null and void. In effect, no authority can pass a law to dissolve Parliament or prorogue it for an election before the end of four years after its first sitting.

Attendance in the House

Electioneering imposes considerable strain and stress on candidates. The work in the House is likely to be disrupted by irregular attendance of Members.

At he commencement of the last meeting of the last session of Parliament, Mr Speaker, Hon. Justice D.F. Annan reminded the House of the heavy agenda before it and the importance of Members' regular attendance to complete the business.

"I am particularly pleased that we have embarked on the final stage of the journey to parliamentary democracy which we began four years ago," said Mr Speaker. "This meeting will be necessarily a short one because of the impending presidential and parliamentary elections. We have a fairly heavy agenda ... and I appeal to Members, in spite of the attractions of the campaign, to ensure that they turn up in their numbers so that the business of this House will not be obstructed by the political campaign, important as the campaign is."

The constitution prescribes the quorum for the business of the House; a lack of quorum means work cannot be done. A quorum of one-third of members is required for the commencement of business; a quorum of not less than one-half of Members is required to determine, for example, a resolution for approval of international loans and a quorum of not less than two-thirds of Members is needed to amend some provisions of the constitution.

The constitution-makers felt that the Legislature should hasten slowly in making laws and that a substantial number of Members should be present to pass them. Therefore the continued absence of a lot of Members from the House would tend to undermine the effective exercise of their legislative functions.

This was a significant problem in the latter days of Parliament during the election campaign. Several key votes had to be postponed until a sufficient number of Members could be persuaded to leave their constituency campaigns and return to Parliament.

This was a significant problem in the latter days of Parliament during the election campaign. Several key votes had to be postponed until a sufficient number of Members could be persuaded to leave their constituency campaigns and return to Parliament.

Self-serving Legislation

An outgoing Parliament may find it a tempting proposition to pass self-serving legislation during its last days. For example, opponents of the Constitutional (Amendment) Bill before the House during the election argued that amendments to provisions of the democratic constitution require a strong national consensus especially as the main opposition parties were not represented in the outgoing Parliament.

However, if a ruling party had an overwhelming majority in an existing Parliament and felt strongly that it would serve its best political interest to do so, it could rush a Bill through all its stages and have it enacted within the remaining few days of its life.

Would a new elected Parliament accord respect and reverence to such amendments to the constitution? Or would a new government set about asking a new parliament to repeal them?

A ruling party which sensed it was heading to defeat could even use an existing Parliament and its constitutional powers to annul a n election, extend its life and call new elections, although it would likely have to justify its action before the Supreme Court.

Although this is an unlikely prospect, it is a potential constitutional problem created by the continuation of an existing Parliament during and even after a parliamentary election.

(This article was originally published in the January 1997 issue of *The Parliamentarian* – Journal of the Parliaments of the Commonwealth).

PARLIAMENTARY VETTING OF MINISTERS
The constitution, and not Parliament, is supreme

The opposition stops the Minister of Finance from reading the budget statement and drags the Attorney-General to the Supreme Court over retained Ministers in the second Parliament of Ghana's fourth republic.

The public perception of the first parliament of Ghana's new democracy was that it lacked the virile opposition as the government's main opponents had boycotted the 1992 parliamentary elections. So when the second Parliament was inaugurated on 7 January, with 67 opposition members in a House of 200, the weight of the public expectation was enormous.

Soon after the first sitting began, the public got a taste of things to come. The first sitting was barely half an hour old when the usual cut-and-thrust elements of vigorous debate were in evidence. A lot of sparks flew.

Even before the swearing-in of Members began, the minority group raised an objection against the flags of the ruling National Democratic Congress (NDC) which decorated the Chamber. That the flags were removed was widely viewed as a welcome sign of political maturity.

Again, although the minority agreed to a motion to hold the presidential swearing-in at Independence instead of Parliament House, they insisted that in future the ceremony "must take place in Parliament and before Parliament".

Led by Mr. Joseph Henry Mensah, Minister of Finance in the second republic and an eminent economist, the minority group gave an unmistakable impression that they would keep the government on its toes and that they were motivated to uphold not only the integrity of Parliament but also the authority of the constitution, which both the majority and minority groups had sworn in Parliament to uphold, defend and protect. As Mr Mensah said: "Mr Speaker, the premises of Parliament, including your own office and the whole premises, is the House of Parliament. And it is our (the Minority's) wish that the authority and dignity of Parliament should be affirmed and re-affirmed on every occasion as one of the bulwarks of the freedom and everything should be done to reinforce it."

Storm Over Retained Ministers Stalls Budget

Immediately after the inauguration of the second Parliament, the opposition Shadow Minister for Justice and Attorney-General, Nana Akufo-Addo, raised the question of the status of Ministers of State and Deputy Ministers. The view of the minority group was that, after the dissolution of the first Parliament, all Ministers and Deputy Ministers had ceased to hold office as of 7 January 1997, the date when President Rawlings's second administration was inaugurated.

The view of the minority group was that as as January 7, 1997, the appointees of the first Parliament, like their appointing authority himself, the President, had exhausted their mandate. The view of the majority group was that Ministers and Deputy Ministers, upon the prior approval of Parliament in 1993-1997, continued to exercise their functions at the President's pleasure.

These skirmishes were merely a prelude to what was to come. Barely a month later, on 7 February, an unusual even took place that brought parliamentary, presidential and constitutional issues to a head, thereby forcing participants and onlookers alike to re-examine the lines of demarcation that circumscribe the authority of each institution. On the previous day, the Majority Leader, Hon. Henry Owusu-Acheampong, had informed the House that the government budget statement would be made by retained Minister of Finance, Hon. Kwame Peprah on the next day.

On Budget Day, the galleries were filled to capacity. To the surprise of the packed House, the Majority Leader announced that the budget would not be presented after all. He said that as a result of a writ filed at the Supreme Court by the Minority Leader "restraining Kwame Peprah from performing this important function as a Minister of State, the budget statement could not be made."

The Speaker accordingly ruled that the main business of the day, the presentation of the budget statement, should be withdrawn until the matters raised at the Supreme Court had been determined. Mr Speaker said: "I would prefer that the issues are determined in the House, as a matter for the House, rather than taken outside the House. But since an issue of interpretation has been raised in a writ, clearly the forum for that is not this House but the Supreme Court ... I would advise that since the writ is now pending, and since the writ raises issues of interpretation, we should refrain as much as possible from advancing arguments one way or another, both as a House, in the House and outside the House."

Mr Mensah clearly relished the Speaker's decision and said: "Mr Speaker, in view of the decision just made, I think it will be appropriate that strangers withdraw from the House forthwith". (Uproar). The stranger in question was, of course, the Minister of Finance because, in the view of the minority, he was neither an elected MP nor a Minister approved by parliament. This marked the first time an opposition had succeeded in stopping as substantial a personage as a Minister of Finance from making a budget statement in the House.

Further Legal Action

Earlier on 7 February, the Minority Leader had taken yet another pre-emptive step by issuing a writ against the Attorney-General claiming a declaration that:

> On a true and proper interpretation of the constitution, particularly Articles 57(3), 58(1), (3), 66(1)(a), 100(1), 133(1) and (3) thereof, no person can after 6 January 1997, act as Minister or Deputy Minister of State, without prior approval by the second Parliament of the fourth republic of this appointment.

Accordingly, any person who has not been so approved and appointed cannot lawfully act or hold himself out as a Minister or Deputy Minister of State.

A copy of the writ with its accompanying affidavit was made available to the Speaker. The withdrawal of the budget may well have been a premature triumph for the minority group.

On 10 February, the President informed the Speaker by letter that he (the President) had decided to retain some of his former Ministers of State.

The minority pointed out that "retention" of Ministers was not consistent with the constitution, which requires that all Ministers should have the prior approval of Parliament before they are appointed. The minority stressed that "retention" was not synonymous with "appointment". The concept had no place within the scheme of the appointment process outlined in the constitution, and therefore no legal effect could be given to it.

In a bid to resolve the argument and perhaps to put all parliamentary action on temporary hold pending the court's deliberations, Mr Mensah had taken out a writ asking the Supreme Court to give a true and proper interpretation of certain provisions of the constitution, particularly in relation to appointment of Ministers of State.

On 13th February, the Minority Leader wrote to the Speaker: "I would be very grateful if you would confirm that in submitting the names ... of his own cabinet, the President was inviting Parliament to exercise its power of prior approval of their appointment as Ministers. I am seeking this confirmation in order to be assured that no action in Parliament is taken which in any way prejudices the determination of the constitutional issues raised in my writ of which you have notice."

The Speaker responded with despatch: "My reading of the express words of the letter from the President's Office leads me to the view that all the names of the persons proposed, whether they are retained Ministers or newly nominated Ministers, were submitted to the House for the purpose of the discharge of the House's constitutional responsibilities in relation to the approval or rejection of Ministers which remain entirely within the competence and authority of the House. I agree that no action may be taken in Parliament which in terms of the Standing Orders prejudices the determination of the constitutional issues raised in your writ which is now pending before the Supreme Court."

Considering the Approval Process
Following the President's declared intention to retain seven Ministers, one of whom was Kwame Peprah, the Speaker referred the nominees to the Appointments Committee.

In accordance with Standing Order No. 172(2), it is the duty of the Appointments Committee of the House to recommend to Parliament for approval or otherwise persons nominated by the President for appointment as Ministers and Deputy Ministers of State.

The committee deliberated on 13 February on the procedure for approving retained or continuing Ministers of State nominated by the President. On the next day, the committee, chaired by

Hon. Ken Dzirasah, who is also the First Deputy Speaker, submitted its report to the House.

The committee decided that where an incumbent Minister or Deputy Minister is retained by the President, it should not be necessary, in view of the previous parliamentary approval, for him or her to appear before the Appointments Committee to be recommended to Parliament for approval or otherwise.

The House adopted the Committee's decision in the form of a resolution. The minority group walked out of the Chamber without voting on the resolution.

On 18 February, the Chairman of the Business Committee informed the House that the Minister of Finance, Mr Peprah, would make his budget statement the following day. When Mr Speaker announced this on the budget day, the Minority Leader stated that he had filed a motion for an interim injunction restraining certain persons including Mr Peprah from acting or holding themselves as Ministers and expressed the hope that the House would be guided by the action.

The Speaker said that he had taken notice of the writ but that the business arranged for the day would be taken. While the House was debating the Sessional Address, Mr Peprah entered the Chamber to present his budget.

The Minority Leader then informed the Speaker that his group needed a few minutes to consult among themselves. They withdrew from the Chamber but remained on the precincts of the House to listen to the budget statement.

The Majority Leader drew attention of the House to Article 117 of the Constitution which provided that "no civil or criminal process coming from any court or place out of Parliament shall be served on, or executed in relation to, the Speaker or a Member or the Clerk to Parliament while he is on his way to, attending at or returning from any proceedings of Parliament". Therefore he said, the matter should not have come before the House at all. He pointed out that the House had already adopted a resolution on the retained Minister.

The Speaker said that following the adoption of the Resolution of the House, he had presented the list of Ministers approved by the House to the President. He added that on that basis the President had authorized the Minister of Finance to present the budget.

"I don't see how the action at the court could stop the House from its legitimate business," said the Speaker. He subsequently ruled that Mr Peprah should make the budget statement.

It was later discovered that the interim injunction notice by the minority had never been listed for hearing, and Mr Peprah had the opportunity to make his budget statement. Notwithstanding the protest, the minority group decided to participate in the debate on the annual estimates and the passage of the Appropriation Bill in the Chamber.

Into the Supreme Court

On 4 March, the minority group pursued its writ, which was amended as follows:

"A necessary incident of prior approval is the consideration and vetting of each nominee for ministerial appointment by the second Parliament for the fourth republic."

The Supreme Court was called upon to determine:

Whether the term of office of Ministers and Deputy Ministers of State appointed by the first President of the fourth republic ended on 7 January 1997;

Whether prior approval of the second Parliament of the fourth republic is required before a Minister or Deputy Minister of State is appointed;

Whether a necessary incident of prior approval is the consideration and vetting of each nominee for ministerial appointment by the second Parliament of the fourth republic;

Whether the requirement of prior parliamentary approval extends to all persons, whether new or retained Ministers and Deputy Ministers, and

Whether prior approval is "a term of art" and if so, what meaning can be attached to it.

An early resolution of the matters raised at the Supreme Court was necessary to avoid the minority and majority groups being set on another confrontational course.

The Majority was determined to walk out on retained Ministers who would appear before the House to introduce Bills, answer Questions or to make statements or motions. They felt that to indulge such Ministers would be to condone illegality.

The Majority, while conceding the right of the minority to

have their say, were equally determined to have their own way. In all, the minority group staged five walkout before and after the Supreme Court had ruled on retained Ministers. The work in the House was disrupted on each occasion. The nation became nervous about political stability, a fundamental element of good governance which had eluded two previous republics.

Both Sides Claim Victory

On 28 May, the Supreme Court ruled on the case by the minority group challenging the constitutional status of retained Ministers in the second Parliament of the Fourth Republic.

The Court, by a unanimous decision, ruled that "every presidential nominee for ministerial appointment, whether retained or new, requires the prior approval of Parliament". Thus the Court upheld the contention of the minority group that by the combined effect of articles 58(1), (2) and (4), 78(1) and (2), 79(1) and (2), 80, 97(1), 100(1) and 113(1) of the 1992 constitution, the tenure of office of a Minister or Deputy Minister is coterminous with the term of the President and the Parliament. And that on expiry of the term of the President and the Parliament, the tenure of the Minister or Deputy Minister also comes to an end.

Accordingly, on the inauguration of a fresh term of a President a Parliament, all Ministers and Deputy Ministers nominated for office need the prior approval of that new Parliament irrespective of whether the nominees was a Minister or Deputy Minister in the previous term.

The court, however, decided by a majority of four to one that the term "prior approval" is not a term of art. In other words, "prior approval" does not connote "consideration and vetting and that no court can question how Parliament goes about exercising its powers of approval. On the other hand, the court held the view by a majority of four to one that "a newly inaugurated Parliament cannot immediately be ready with its various committees to approve presidential nominees."

The impasse over the retained Ministers deepened as both the minority and majority groups claimed victory over the Supreme Court rulings. The minority insisted that all Ministers, including the hold-over Ministers, had to receive the prior approval of Parliament and that Parliament had its own procedure for approving ministerial nominees of the President which should be adhered to. As far as it was concerned, the resolution of 14 February that it was not necessary for incumbent Ministers and Deputies to go through the approval process again contravened Parliament's own Standing Orders.

On the other hand, the majority group felt that, since "prior approval" is not a term of art, the resolution of 14 February was still valid as the House should adopt its own method of approval which no court could question.

A Way Through the Stand-Off

There was considerable public pressure on Parliament to resolve the impasse which had resulted in walkouts that were disrupting the work in the House.

The opposition indicated that it would table a motion to rescind the 14 February resolution. Worried by opposition walkouts which could determine the credibility of the House, the Majority put forward suggestion to the Minority to arrive at a consensus motion for debate in the House. Both sides were now willing to accommodate each other. On 8 July, the following motion was debated in the House:

> That the resolution of 14 February 1997 be reviewed and that any person nominated by the President for reappointment as Minister or Deputy Minister shall have prior approval of Parliament in accordance with the rules of the House and that prior approval is not a term of art.

The motion stood in the names of Majority and Minority Leaders. In a conciliatory tone, the Majority Leader said that *"ti Koro nnko agyina"*, an Akan proverb which freely translated means it is always better to have two heads to deliberate upon an issue in order to arrive at a decision.

"The fact that we have a respectable opposition in the House today, the fact that we are able to cooperate with them on important matters of state, is something that really this whole nation should be proud of," he said.

In seconding the motion, the Minority Leader quoted another Akan proverb: *"Se ye wirefi, na yesan kofa a, yenkyi"*, which literally translated means that if you are going on a journey and you remember you have left something behind, it is no shame to go back and collect it.

The Minority Leader said that it was worthwhile to celebrate a great victory in the second Parliament of the fourth republic, a victory for both sides of the House. Indeed, as he put it, it was a victory for Parliament that in the end the leadership of the House had been able to guide it to a principled, yet at the same time politically viable, solution.

The motion was agreed unanimously and the opposition decided to do business in the House.

Reflections on the Impasse

Many people, including the Speaker, expressed unhappiness with the minority group walking out of the proceedings in Parliament. During the Fifth South African Workshop, organised by the Commonwealth Parliamentary Association, the issue of boycotts in Parliament received lively discussion. It was noted that in a few countries the opposition too easily tended to resort to this tactic to draw attention to their protests. Even in Namibia, we understand that the current Majority, let by the Prime Minister, walked out in protest against a ruling from the Chair.

Sir Norman Manley, who was at different times Prime Minister and Leader of Opposition in Jamaica, made the following pertinent observation on opposition boycotts:

> The boycott is obviously a revolutionary gesture born of frustration and despair of success by any conventional means. As a rule, it is valuable only if it is accompanied by other and more overtly violent activities born of the same situation. By itself and in a country with organised parties and actively based on democratic procedures, it is clearly out of place. It could result in defeating its own objectives, leaving the government serenely in power, and destroying the hopes of the followers of the opposition party.

K.B. Ayensu, the first Clerk of Parliament of independent Ghana, whose sudden death on 17 June 1997 was a sad loss to Parliament, observed that this type of boycott was sharply distinguishable from other forms of limited but extreme protest designed to highlight proper objectives and attract the maximum of public attention. After all, it was the heart and soul of politics to succeed in being noticed.

It is my opinion that Parliament is the proper forum for political parties to make their policies and programmes known. They are privileged to discuss openly and freely and without fear whatever they wish in the House. However, in matters of a constitutional nature or interpretation, the Supreme Court is the appropriate forum to settle issues. The minority groups in Ghana and elsewhere felt that participation in proceedings of the House involving the interpretation of the constitution was an exercise in illegality.

Supremacy of the Constitution and Consensus

The approach taken by the Supreme Court and the House itself to resolve the impasse underlined the fact that the constitution is the supreme law of the country. Indeed, the constitution-framers of 1969, 1979 and 1992 each prescribed a Parliament with limited legislative powers.

Article 93(2) of the 1992 constitution makes it clear that although Parliament is vested with legislative powers, such powers must be exercised subject to the provisions of the constitution. For example, short of amending the constitution, there is no procedure available to Parliament by which it can pass a law making Ghana a one-party state. Any law passed by Parliament which is inconsistent with any provision of the Constitution can be challenged in the Supreme Court, which may declare such law null and void.

It is often said that Parliament is master of its own procedure. Article 110 of the constitution does allow Parliament to regulate its proceedings. But procedures adopted by Parliament must not contravene any of the provisions of the constitution. These measures were adopted by the constitution-framers against the backdrop of the nation's past experiences.

Although procedures are not sacrosanct, the enduring quality of the procedure is an important factor in its credibility and authority. Procedures should not therefore be amended at will or at the whim of the majority.

The Minority Spokesman for Justice and Attorney-General summed up the importance of the consensus motion. He said: "The first point is that Ministers and Deputy Ministers are in office for a limited period of time, their tenure of office being conterminous with the life of the President and Parliament that appointed them.

"Second, it is the duty of Parliament alone to approve the appointment of Ministers and Parliament does not share this power with any organ of state."

The compromise motion also emphasised the need for Parliament to decide certain matters of national importance, such as the economy and defence and foreign policies, by consensus rather than party strength.

Early Ministerial Appointments

The constitution provides a hybrid system of government, a blend of presidential and parliamentary systems. In the parliamentary system, Ministers and Deputy Ministers of State do not require parliamentary approval for their prior appointment. The cabinet is announced within hours of their election to Parliament.

In the case of the presidential system, our constitution provides that parliamentary approval is required for appointment of Ministers and Deputy Ministers. To avoid delays in the ministerial appointments , it is suggested that the President should compose his core cabinet for early consideration by Parliament. It may not be possible to announce all the Ministers at once, but it is good practice for the core of cabinet to be already in office before the State Opening of Parliament by the President.

It is to the credit of Ghana's parliamentary democracy that both the minority and majority groups were able to tolerate the uncertainty of an untested issue and that they exercised political maturity to reach a consensus on a potentially divisive matter of national importance.

The Speaker cogently expressed the general mood of the nation when he said the consensus reached was a victory for democracy, a victory for Parliament and victory for the nation.

(This article was originally published on the October 1997 issue of *The Parliamentarian,* Journal of Parliaments of the Commonwealth).

The Presidents/Prime Ministers

First President Dr. Kwame Nkrumah
18th July, 1960 – 24th Feb. 1966
Prime Minister 1957-60

Prime Minister Prof K.A. Busia
September 1969 – 13th January 1972

President Edward Akufo-Addo
October, 1969 – 13th January, 1972

President Dr. Hilla Lemann
September 1979 – 31 December, 1981

President Flt. Lt. J.J. Rawlings
7th Jan. 1993 – 6th Jan. 2000

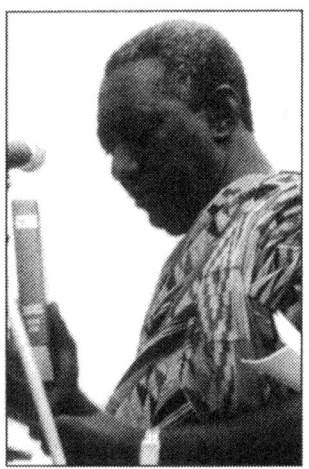
President J.A. Kufuor
7th Jan. 2001 to date

The Speakers of Parliament

First Speaker
Hon. Sir Emmanuel Charles Quist, KT
March, 1951 – November, 1957

Second Speaker
Hon. Justice Augustus Molode Akiwumi
November, 1957 – June 1960

Third Speaker
Hon. Joseph Richard Asiedu
July, 1960 – June, 1965

Fourth Speaker
Hon. Kofi Asante Ofori Atta
10th June, 1965 – 24 February 1966

Fifth Speaker
Rt. Hon. Justice Nii Ama Ollenu
September 1969 – 13th Jan. 1972

Sixth Speaker
Rt. Hon. Justice Jacob Hademburg Griffiths-Randolph
24th Sep. 1979 – 31 Dec. 1981

Seventh Speaker
Rt. Hon. Justice Daniel Fancis Annan
7th Jan. 1993 – 6th Jan. 2001

Eighth Speaker
Rt. Hon. Peter Ala Adjetey
7th Jan. 2001 to 6th Jan. 2005

Ninth Speaker
Rt. Hon. Begyina Sakyi-Hughes
7th Jan. 2005 to date

Index

Abacha, Sani Gen. 84, 85
Abban, A.S.A. 50
Abavana, L.R. 34, 54
Abdul-Saaka, M. Hon. 61
Abedi A.A. Hon. 61
Abingya Simon Hon. 73, 83
Ablo, Edmond Hon. Dr. 66
Aboagye, E.K. Hon. 74
Aboagye Kwesi Hon. 83
Abodakpi, Dan Hon. 73, 82
Abofour, Offinso District 12
Aborigene's Rights Protection Society (1897) 18, 22
Abrefa R. Owusu Ansah 67
Abu, John Hon. Dr. 73, 81
Abulu, Godfrey Hon. 72
Acheampong, Owusu J.H. Hon. 74
Achuliwor, Sefuni Hon, 103
Acquah, Francis Dr. 67
Action Congress Party 67
Acts of Parliament 112, 119
Acts of Parliament see also individual Acts
    e.g. Criminal (Amendment) Act 1995
Ad Hoc Committees 126, 127
Adabre, Donald, Hon. 74, 82
Adade, N.Y.B. Hon. 60
Adam, Eben Hon 55
Adam, Ibrahim Hon 72
Adama, B.K. Hon. 35, 61
Adamafio Nii Okaija, Hon 81
Adamafio Tawiah 42
Adamu S.P Hon. 74, 83
Adda, Joseph Kofi 135
Addae-Gyamera, Kwaku 73
Addo-Kufour Kwame Hon. Dr. 101
Adinkra Symbols 47
Adisadel 23
Adjaho, E.K. Doe Hon. 103
Adjei, Ako E. Hon. 22, 25, 34, 39, 42
Adjei-Darko, Kwadwo Hon. 101
Adjei-Kwabena, Hon. Dr. 73, 81
Adjei-Mensah, Isaac K. Hon. 73, 81, 103
Adjetey Peter Ala Rt. Hon. 103, 104
Administration of Justice 123
Adow, Patience Hon. Miss 82
Aduhene, W.K. 51
Afful, J.E. Hon. 81
Afigya Sekyere East 118
Africa 59, 75
    Anglophone 78

    Francophone 78
    Total Liberation of 22
African Common Currency 23
African Common Market 23
African Continental Parliamentary Association 59
African Emancipation 22
African High Command 22, 23
African Liberation Front 23
African Morning Post 21
African Morning Post see also Gold Coast Spectator, the
African Olympiad 23
"African Personality" 47
African Revolution 57, 58
Afrifa, A.A. HE. Brig. 62, 63
Afriyie, Kwaku, Hon. Dr. 101
Agama, John G.K. Hon. 61, 71, 104
Agamemnon Legendary King of Argos 28
Agbenaza, C.K. Hon. Lt. Col. 82
Aggrey, Joe Hon. 103
Aggrey John King of Cape Coast 15, 19, 20
Aggrey-Orleans, J.E.K. 67
Agomila, Adombilla Hon. Dr. 102
Agriculture 76, 87
Agume, Daniel 67
Agyei, Akwasi Osei Hon. 102
Agyekum, Daniel O. Hon. 73, 82
Agyekum, K.P. Hon. 61
Agyekum, Owusu Dr. 74
Agyemang-Duah, Baffour Dr. 10
Ahedor, Victor Atsu 74
Ahiable Modestus Hon. 73
Ahwoi, Kwamena Hon. 73, 81
Aidoo, A.O. Hon. 103
Aidoo Joseph Boahen Hon. 102, 135
Akanbodiipo Lydia A. 61
Akita, Edward Hon. 102
Akiwumi, A.M. 39, 46, 47
Akomea, Nana Hon. 103
Akorli, Steve S. Hon. 82
Akorsah, G.K. Hon. Dr. 73
Akoto, Bafour Osei 20, 27
Akufo-Addo Edward Hon. Justice 22, 25, 60
Akufo-Addo Nana Addo Dankwa Hon. 101, 134, 144
Akuffo Alex Hon. 83
Akuffo F.W.A. Dr. 66
Akumfi, Christopher Ameyaw Prof. Hon. 101, 135

Akushie, Dan. 74
Al-Hassan, Malik Yakubu Hon. 101
Al-Hassan Sussana Hon. 46, 55
Alabi Joshua Hon. 82
All Peoples Republican Party 62
Allasani, J.H. Hon. 34
Amamoo, J.G. Hon. 61
Amandi Adam Hon. 61
Amankwah, D.K. Hon. 72
American Constitution 117
American Presidential System 119, 121, 124
Ametepeh, Daniel 104
Amidu, Martin Hon. 73, 82
Amissah-Aidoo, Isaac Hon. 61, 62
Amissah-Arthur K.B. 73
Amoa-Awuah, K. 34, 55
Amoako-Atta, K. 54, 58
Amoako-Atta, R.O. 34, 50, 55
Amoako-Nuamah, Christine Dr. Hon. Mrs. 72, 81
Amofa, Owuraku Hon. 82
Amonoo Chief of Anumabo (1844) 15
Amoro, W.A. 51
Ampaw S.D. Hon. 60
Amponsah, R.R. Hon. 27, 60
Amua-Awuah, K. Hon. 34, 55
Amugi, J.O. 67
Anaba, Faisal 74
Anane Adjei N. Hon. 55
Anane, Richard Winfred Hon. Dr. 101
Andzie-Quainoo Liz 10
Anin, Lucy 46
Anin, P.D. Justice 11-12
Annan, Daniel Francis Rt. Hon. 71, 74, 83, 84, 89, 140
Annan, Kofi UN Sec. Gen. 78, 86
Annan, Mcjewells 10
Anti-Inflation Committee 28
Anti, K.K. Hon. 60
Antuban, Kofi 47
Antwi D.K. Hon. Dr. 102
Antwi-Kubi A. Hon. 61
Apaloo, Fred Chief, Justice 71
Apaloo, M.K. 39
Appiah-Dwomoh, Joana Mrs. 74, 83
Appiah, Joe 27, 97
Appiah, Menka A. Hon. 61
Appointments Committee 128, 129, 146
 on Ministerial nominations 90
Appointments of Ministers see Ministers of State, appointments of
Appraku, Kofi Konadu Hon. Dr. 101
Appropriation Bill 148
Approval processes 146

Arden-Clarke, Charles Sir 28, 31
Arkaah, Kow Nkensen HE 72
Armah Kwesi Hon. 55, 58
Armed Forces 9, 65
 and Police 64
Armed Forces see also Ghana Armed Forces
Armed Forces Revoluntionary Council 68
 members of 70
 suspense Account 68
Armed Rebellion 122
Arthur, Emmanuel 66
Arthur, John 34
Arthur, S.B. Hon. Dr. 74, 75
Arthur, S.G. 67
Asabigi, Nassamu Hon. 83
Asamany, Regina Hon. 46
Asamoah, Comfort Hon. 46
Asamoah, Obed Hon. Dr. 72, 83
Asante, K.K. 66
Asante, S.K.B. Dr. 71, 124
Asante, W.B. 74
Asare, F.Y. 34, 50
Asenta 21
Ashanti, Region 46
Ashitey Ismael Hon. 102
Asiedu, Richard Joseph Hon. 39, 51
Asmah, Gladys Hon. Mrs. 83, 101
Associated Negro Press Incorporated of Chicago 28
Asumada, Ayeebo 34, 50, 55
Attorney-General and Minister for Justice, 42, 83, 124, 143, 144, 152
Auditor-General
 reports on Accounts 127
Australia, 131
Avoka Cletus Hon. 81
Awoonor Kofi Hon Prof. 81
Awoonor-Williams, F. 22
Awoosie, Chief of Domenase 15
Awuku-Darko, S.W. Hon. 60
Awuni, L.M. 67
Ayensu, Grace 46
Ayensu, Kobina B. 9, 11, 12, 21, 22, 31, 35, 38, 39, 42, 43, 45, 47, 51, 56, 59, 80, 96, 97, 138
Ayidiya, S.A. Hon. Dr. 73
Ayiribi-Acquah, E.A. Dr. 74
Azikiwe, Nnamdi 21
Baah, Kwaku, Hon. 61
Baah, Moses Hon. 103
Baah-Wiredu, Kwadwo Hon. 101, 134
Baako, Kofi Hon. 35, 50, 52, 56
Baba, A.A. 67

Backbenchers 38, 47, 96, 123
Bagbin A.S.K. Hon. 103
Bamba, Moctar Hon. Atta 102
Bank of Ghana 53
Bannerman, Cecilia Hon. Mrs. 101
Bannerman, James 17
Bannerman, S. 16
Barimah, Yaw Hon. 102, 135
Barnett, Claude 28
Bart-Plange, Jacob Kwesi 27
Bartels, Kwamena Hon. 102, 135
Bawa Rashid, Hon. 103
Bawumia, Mumuni Hon. 55
Bediako, A. 66
Bempah, Kofi Owusu Dr. 67
Beninbengor-Blay 51,55
Benneh, George Hon. Prof. 65, 70, 90
Benneh J.W. 55
Bensah, E.K. 34, 50, 54, 56
Bentim, Charles 134
Bentum, B.A. 55
Benyiwa-Doe, Ama Hon. Mrs. 82
Big Six 25
Big Six see also Adjei, Ako E, Obetsebi-Lamptey, Nkrumah, Kwame, Akufo-Addo Edward Ofori-Atta William, Dankwa, J.B. Dr.
Bilijo, Moses Nayong Hon. 82
Bills 112, 114, 120, 125, 127, 128, 129
Bills see also individual Bill's
Bing Geoffrey 41
Blake 23
Blankson, Kuntu 21
Blay F.W.A. Hon. 103, 104
Blay F.W.K. Hon. 83, 84
Blay R.S. Hon. 22, 59
Boafo, Sampson Kwaku Hon. 83, 102, 135
Boateng, Akuamoa Hon. Justice 61
Boateng D.S. Hon. 72, 82
Boateng, Kwaku Hon. 50
Bond of 1844, 15, 18, 19, 26, 29, 36, 48
    basis of British Jurisdiction in the Gold Coast 15
Bonful Kwaku, A 74
Boni Hans, Kofi Hon. 55
Bonsu, Kwaku, S.A. 51, 55
Bonsu, Osei Kyei-Mensah Hon. 103
Bosumtwi-Sam, Albert Hon. 82
Botsio, Kojo Hon. 30, 33, 34, 36, 50, 54, 56
Botwe, Dan 135
Botchwey, Kwesi Hon. Dr. 72
Boycotts 25
    in Parliament 151
Braimah, Farouk Hon. Dr. 73, 83

Breaches of Privileges
    sanctions on 108
British Broadcasting Corporation (BBC) 97, 98
British Commonwealth of Nations 30, 37
British Government 27, 29
British Members of Parliament 80
British Officers 20, 24
British Overseas Airways Corporation 32
British Parliament 75
British Parliament see also House of Commons
British Settlements Acts 1887 and 1945, 31
Brodie-Mends, T.D. Hon. 60
Brong-Ahafo Region 46
Brookman-Amissah, Eunice Dr. Mrs. 81
Bruce-Konuah W.G. Hon. Dr. Mrs. 60
Buah, F.K. Hon. 66
Budget 58, 70, 71, 91, 116, 121, 123, 143, 144, 145, 147
    day 58
    1964 113
    1993 76
    statement 147
Bugase, Clement, Hon. 82
Bullah Vincent W. 66
Burke Edmund 37
Busia, Kofi Abrefa Prof. 16, 34, 37, 60, 64, 65
    administration 71
Business
    Golden age of 105
Business Committee 126, 127, 128, 129, 132, 147
Buslamante 92,
Butler, R.A. 31
Bye-election 104
Bye-election see also Elections
Cabinet 114, 115, 153
Cairo, Egypt 58
Cape Coast 19, 20
Castle 15
Carnarvon, Earl of 19
Casely-Hayford, Archie 33
Cash and Carry
    abolition of 107
Castle 15
    seat of Government 109
Cedi devaluation 64
Centre for Democratic Development (CDD) 110
Certificate of Urgency 41, 113, 127
Chambas, Mohammed Ibn Hon. Dr. 74, 82
Chapman C.H. 39
Charles I King of England 75, 93

Cheetham, James Henry 17
Chiana Pio see also Pe, Roland Ayagitan
Chief Justice 42, 60, 71
Chief Justice see also Supreme Court
Chief Whip 45
Chiefs 77
Chinebuah, Isaac K Hon. Dr. 55, 65
Chireh, Yileh Hon. 73
Churcher, Christian Hon. Ms. 101
Churchill, Winston 18, 38
Citizenship, dual 77
Civil Servants, Senior 125
Civil Service Commission 42
Cleland George 17
Clerk of Parliament 11, 21, 33, 39, 51, 54, 59, 93, 96-97, 118, 131, 138, 147
 confrontation with Governor 31
Cocoa 76
Cocoa Farmers
 Ashanti/Brong Ahafo 27
Cocoa Producer Prices 65, 70
Coleman Grace Hon. Mrs. 102
Colonial Government 25
Colonial Office 25, 26, 29
Commission of Enquiry 25
 and Constitutional Committee 25-26
Committees
 after First Republic 127
 chairmen of 129
 first Parliament 126,128
 Fourth Parliament 127
 meetings of 130 of members holding offices of Profit 128
 of members holding public offices 129
 of whole House 130
 on government assurances 128
 members of reflects party strengths on
  the House 129
 of experts on Constitutional proposal for 1992 Constitution 124
 powers of 131-132
 select see also Select Committees
 size of 129
 strengths of 129
 system 119, 122
  advantages of 132-133
  development of 125-126
Commons, House of see House of Commons
Commonwealth 12, 29, 36, 40, 49, 57
 Secretariat 12, 65
Commonwealth Parliamentary Association 40, 138

Compaore, Blaise 104
Conference of Heads of States and Governments see Organisation of African Unity.
Conflict resolutions in Africa 22
Congress 116
 of British West Africa 18
 system of Government 123
 United States of America 125
Constituent Assembly 12, 65, 117
Constituent Assembly and Plebiscite Act 1960 41
Constitution 30, 44, 71
 1957 112
 1960 16, 112
 1969 59, 64, 113, 114-116, 117, 120, 121, 127, 147
  article 117, 147
 1979 65, 113, 115, 116-117, 121
 1992 Draft 72, 117
 1992 10, 71, 77, 78, 80, 100, 113, 115, 122
  article 57 (3) 145
  58 (1) (2) (4) 91, 145, 149
  78, 122
  78 (1) & (2) 88, 91, 149
  66 (1) 145
  79 (1) & (2) 91, 149
  80 91
  93 (2) 152
  97 (1) 91, 145
  100 (1) 9, 149,
  103, 129, 131
  108 122
  110 152
  113 (1) 80, 91, 123, 124, 139, 149
  133 (1) & (3) 145
  amending the 152
  framers of the 153
  supremacy of the 152-153
  weakness in the previous 121
Constitutional (Amendment) Bill 141
Constitutional Commission 59
Constitutional Practice
 a remedy for past maladies 140
 attendance in the House 140-141
 following a different practice 139
 self-serving legislation 141
Constitutional proposals 60
Constitutional rule 117
Consultative Assembly 71 117
 1992 117
Contempt of Court 42
Contempt of Parliament
 Complaints of 126

Conventions Peoples Party (CPP) 9, 23, 26, 35, 27, 29, 30, 39, 40, 43, 44, 46, 51, 60, 63, 84, 96, 97, 104, 134
Coomah, Chibboe Chief of Assin 15
Corruption 64, 106
Council of State
  Member of 64
Coup de' tat 63
  1958 58
  24 Feb. 66 11
  31st Dec. 1981 117
Courts 44, 115
  Special 42
Courts see also Supreme Court
Coussey, Henley Justice Sir 26
Coussey Report 26
Crabbe, Cofie 42
Crabbe, VCRAC Justice 65
Creasy Gerald Sir 25
Criminal (Amendment) Act 1995 78
Criminal Libel Law 107
Criminal (repeal of Criminal Libel Law and Seditious Laws) (Amendment) Bill 109
Cross Roads 24-25 29
Cudjoe, Chibboe King of Denkera 15
Cudjoe Sam Hon. 66
Da Costa, Aboagye A.A Hon. 61
Da Costa Kankam 66
Dadam Kojo Maama 74
Dado Johnson Hon. 66
Dadson E.K. 50
Dadzie, Francis Hon. 65
Dadzie Kweku (steel) 20
Dalgleish, A 25
Dame Grand Cross
  Most excellent Order of the British Empire 35
Dame Grand Cross of
  Royal Victorian Order 35
Daniels, Ekow Hon. Dr. 55, 65
Danquah, Ampem 74, 107
Danquah, J.B. Hon. Dr. 20, 23, 25, 26, 28, 41, 43, 48, 62, 107
Dapaah, Albert Kan 102, 135
Darko-Sarkwa, R. 51
Darkwa, S.N. 9, 12, 56, 62, 67, 74, 75, 80, 83, 84, 90
Davidson, Rachel 31
De Graft, Dickson 34, 50
De Graft Johnson 68
De Graft Johnson J.SE. 22, 65, 67, 68, 74, 83
De Montford Parliament 58
De Montfort Peter 58

De Montford, Simon 93
Debate 109, 113, 115, 120, 123, 150
  Rules of 131
Debrah, Ernest A Hon. 102, 135
Defence 123
Defence see also Armed Forces
Democracy 105
Democracy see also Parliamentary Democracy,
  Peoples Socialist Democracy
Democratic Peoples Party 118
Democratic Procedures 151
Deportation (Indemnity) Bill, 1958
Deportation Order 41
Dery Ambrose 135
Detention Law 43
Detention Law see also Preventive Detention Act
Detention of the Big Six see Big Six
Disease 106
Dissolution of Parliament 123
Dissolution of Parliament see Parliament, Dissolution
District Assemblies 118
  Common Fund 87
District Commissioners, British 25
Diversification Programme 87
Divestiture Programme 76
Documents
  Departmental 131
Dodoo, S.O. 62, 74, 83
Doe, E.K. 35
Doku, Sophia Hon. 46
Dombo, S.D. Hon. 33, 38, 48, 60
Dometey, Narh Hon. 103
Donkor, E.KT. Hon. Lt-Col. 82
Donkor Joe Hon. 103
Donkor, Nuamah Hon. 74, 82
Donkor, T.A. 66
Dougan, Kwesi 67
Dowuona-Hammond AJ Hon. 50, 54
Draft Constitution 30
Duchess of Kent 31, 32, 35
Duffour, Adjei Hon. 103
Duke of Norfolk 31
Delimitation Commission 54
Dwomoh, Joana Appiah Hon. Mrs. 83
Dzamesi Kofi Hon. 103, 135
Dzirasah, Kenneth Hon. 74, 83, 84, 90, 103, 147
Dzirasah S.A. Rev. 50
Eastern Region 46
Economy 63, 75, 76, 153
Edumadze, Isaac Eduasar Hon. 102

Edusei, Krobo Hon. 33, 34, 41, 42, 50
Effa-Dartey Nkrabea Hon. Capt. (rtd) 102
Egala Imoru Hon. 54
Egle Party 77, 117, 118,
Ekuban J.E. Hon. 73
Elections 12, 26, 69, 80, 81, 95, 100, 115, 123, 139, 140, 153
   campaign period 80
   general 100
      1954 29
      1956 29, 30
      1979 65
      2000 109
      1992 72, 143,
      1996 85
   Multi-party 10
   Parliamentary 72, 75, 77, 141, 143
   Presidential 72, 139, 140
Electoral Commission 85, 139
Electoral process 105
Electorate 92, 108, 123
Eledi, Clement Hon. 103
Emergency Powers 25
Erzuah J.B. Hon. 34
Esseku Haruna Hon. 60
Establishment Secretariat 42
Ex-Service men 25
Executive 94, 114, 116, 121, 122, 124, 125, 126, 132
   independence of the 116
   members of 65, 54, 81, 134-135
   and officers of Parliament 50-51
   President see President
Export Development 87
Exports – Non traditional 87
Eyadema, Gnassingbe HE 104
Farmer George 18
Farms 75
Fante Confederacy of (1868) 18
Fante Cultural Tradition 20
Fante Fekuw Society (1885) 18
Federation of Youth Organisations 35
Felton, Stanley 10
Finance and Economic Planning, Min. of 70
Finance Committee 128
Finance, Minister of 143, 144, 145, 147
Financial Measures 126
Financial Policy-Government 58, 70, 91
First Republic see Ghana, First Republic 52
Fitih C.C. 70
Five Year Development Plan 87
Flagstaff House 43, 96
Fobih, Dominic Kwaku Hon. Prof. 101, 135
Food and Agriculture
   Committee on 131
Foot, Dingle 25
Foreign Affairs 58, 123
Foreign goods
   Boycott of 25
Foreign Jurisdiction Act 31
Foreign Policy 153
Forson, A.K. Hon. 72
Forson Amy Olga Ms. 104
Forts and Settlements
   on the Gold Coast 17
Fosu, E.K. Hon. 73
Fosu Kwabena Hon. 82
Fourth Republic see Ghana Fourth Republic
Free Trade 20
Freedom and Justice 75, 98
Freedom of Speech 94
Fuseini, B.A. Hon. Alhaji 74
Fynn J.R. Hon. Dr. 61
Gamey, Austin A. Hon. 82
Gbagbo, Laurent 104
Gbedemah, K.A. Hon. 26, 30, 33, 34, 50
Gbeho, James, Victor Hon. 83
Gebre, Second Chief of Assin 15
General Elections see Elections, general
Geneva, Switzerland 39
George III King of England 18
George V Memorial Hall 32
Ghana Armed Forces 58
Ghana
   at 40 98
   Congress System of Government 119-122
   Constitution Order in Council 1957 37
   Constitution see under constitution
   Cross Roads Tragedy 24-25
   First Republic 51, 52, 54, 58, 59, 79, 119, 127
      First Parliament 118, 54
      Parliament under 113,-114
   Fourth Republic 12, 77-81, 110, 119, 125
      First Parliament 72, 104, 117, 118, 139
      Fourth Parliament 2000 134
      State opening of second Parliament 86
      Third Parliament 10, 100, 108, 109
   Indebtedness 63
   Independence 9, 10, 24, 28, 29, 40, 44, 49, 69, 100, 124, 154
      Act 1957 31, 36

bill 30, 31
Constitution 1957 see
Constitution
   Day 31
   golden Jubilee 99
   National Anthem 33
   43rd 105, 106
   40th 98
   Vigil 33
   Second Republic 59, 64-65, 117, 119,- 120, 121, 125
   First sitting of Parliament 84
   First Parliament State Opening 62-64
   Third Republic 65, 70, 116, 124, 125
   inauguration of 67-70
   constitution 119
   Trek to Nationhood 18-21
   Vision 2020 87
Ghana Investment Bank 53
Ghana National College 23, 27
Ghana National Trading Company 64
Ghana Political Existence 45
Ghann, J.Y. Hon. 55
Gizo, M.A. Hon. 73
Goka, F.K.D. Hon. 34, 50
Gold Coast 9, 16, 28, 30, 32
   1850–1957 9
Gold Coast see also Ghana
Gold Coast Chronicle 21
Gold Coast Echo 21
Gold Coast Leader 21
Gold Coast Methodist Times 21
Gold Coast Nation 21
Gold Coast Observer 21
Gold Coast Spectator 21
Government 44, 48, 53, 70, 81, 86, 107, 108, 118, 120, 132, 133
   arms of 114
   good 63
   presidential system of 116
Governor 16, 17, 25, 32, 36
   Versus clerk of Parliament Confrontation 31
Governor, General 38, 41, 48
   assent 45
Governor General of Nigeria 21
Governor, Lieutenant 15,16
Grant, Francis Chapman 17
Grant Paa 22, 23, 24
Great Alliance 118
Great Britain 22, 41, 93
Greater London Council 39
Griffiths, PMG Cdr. 82

Griffiths-Randolph, Jacob Hackenberg Justice 67-68
Guiana,
   Legislative Council of 37
Guinea 68
Gulf War 87
Gumah, Sheriff Hon. 73
Gyamfi K. Dr. 66
HIV/AIDS 107
Hagan J.E. 34, 50, 55
Haizel, E.A. Hon. 50, 66
Hammah, Ekow (Rope) 20
Hammah, Ekow see also Hammond, George
Hammah, Mike, Hon. 82
Hammond George 20
Hammond K.T. Hon. 103
Hansand Official Report 51
Harley, J.W.K. 62
Haroun, Abel-Majeed Hon. Dr. 102
Haruna, Ibrahim Hon. Alhaji 66
Hay Philip 31
Health and Education
   Committee on 130
Health Sector 86
Heritage Party 118
High Court 41
Honer-sam Sophia Hon. 103
House Committee 126, 129
House Committee see Parliament
House of Commons 19, 20, 29, 31, 37, 41, 58, 80, 93, 94, 97
   opening of new 37
   select Committee 19, 20, 130,
   Standing Committee comparison with that of Ghana 128
Human Rights 40, 106
Human Sacrifices 15
Hunger 106
Hutchinson, William 17
Hutton-Mills, Thomas 17
Hybrid System of Government 153
   Central purpose of 122-123, 125
IPU 39
Ibrahim Adbdulai Hon. Lt.-Col. (rtd) 73
Iddi, Gilbert Seidu Hon. 74, 82
Iddris, Mustapha Ali Hon. 102
Iddrisu Mahama Hon. Alh. 72, 81
Iddrisu, S.I. 59
Impasse 150-151
   Reflections on 151-153
Imperialism 26
Indemnity law 42
Independence Ghana see Ghana

Independence
Independent members of Parliament see
Parliament, independent members
Industrial Regulations (Amendment)
   Bill 64
Inflation 92
Inkumsah, A.E. Hon. 34, 50, 56
Inter Parliamentary Union 1958 39
Interior, Minister of 50, 97
International Finance Corporation 91
International Monetary fund 77
Interpretation 146, 152
   Issue of 144
Investment Code Bill 71
Issah, Ali Yussif Hon. Mallam 102
Jamaica 19, 92
   Leader of opposition 151
Jantuah, F.A. 55
Jantuah S.K.P. Hon. 66
Jebbah, John Hon. 103
Jehu-Appiah Hon. 74, 83
Jewish Council 97
John Paul I Pope 78
Johnson, Mate 51
Johnson, Wallace 21
Judges 42, 98
Judges see also Chief Justice
Judiciary 114
Kaleo Jatoe Hon. 60
Kan-Dapaah, Albert, Hon. 102, 135
Kanda, D.S.K. 62, 67
Kensington Palace 31
Ketekewu, Isaah Hon. 103
Kodzo Joseph Hon. 51, 55
Kofi-Sackey H.W. Hon. 61
Konare, Alpha Omar 104
Konu B.A. Hon. 55
Koranteng, Mary 46
Korbieh, Francis 73
Korboe, E.H.T. Hon. 50
Korsah, Arku Sir 42
Kpodonu, A.S. 56
Krakue, Stephen Hon. 61
Kudadjier J.N. 62
Kufour Benjamin Osei Hon. 103
Kufour John Agyekum HE 61, 85, 100,
   101, 104, 105, 109, 122, 134
   inauguration 10
Kuntu-Blankson, George 17
Kuntu Kofi 20
Kuntu, Kofi see also Blankson, Frank
Kusi Gifty, Eugenia Hon. Mrs. 103
Kwaku, Edward Osei Hon. 102
Kwame Nkrumah Memorial Park 33

Kwame Nkrumah Memorial Park see also
   Nkrumah Kwame Dr. HE
Kwame, Obeng King 29
Kwapong D.A. 10
Kwaw-Swanzy, B.A. 55
Kwegyir Aggrey Dr. 11
Kwesi Margaret Clarke Mrs. 73, 81
Kwofie James Ampah 67
Kyere, Kwabena Hon. 73, 82
Kyeremanteng, Alan Hon. 135
Lamptey, A.L. Col (Rtd) Hon. 104
Lamptey Kwesi Hon. 60
Language indigenous 98
Laryea, A.M. Dr. 74
Leader of the House see Parliament
Leadership 78
Legal action 145
Legislation
   retroactive 42
Legislative Assembly 9, 33, 112
   members of 112
Legislative Assembly see also Parliament
Legislative authority 112
Legislative Council 16, 17, 18, 21, 38
   bye-election 27
   1951 26
   1850 26
Legislative enactments 53
Legislative Instruments 113
Legislative Powers
   on the First President 112, 152
   exercise of, in Ghana 16
Legislative process 115, 127
Legislators see Members of Parliament
Legislature 18, 114, 116, 121, 123, 127, 132,
   141
Lenox-Boyd, Alan 29, 30
Lenthall, K. William 93
Library 123
Listowell, Earl of 47
Limann, Hilla Dr. HE 16, 65, 68, 69, 71
Local Government, Minister of 27, 45, 46
Lokko, C.A. 35, 51, 56, 62
London 65
Lord Chancellor 94
Lord Privy Seal 32
Lords, House of 93, 94
Mace of Parliament of Ghana 15, 47, 131
Maclean George 16, 48
Madjitey E.R.T Hon. 41, 42, 61
Mahama Alima Hon. Ms. 102, 135
Mahama Aliu HE Alhaji 101, 104, 106, 134
Mahama, E.A. Hon. 34, 50, 55
Mahama Edward Dr. 85

Mahama, John D. Hon. 82
Mahama Shani Hon. 61
Mahami, Edmond Dramani 67, 68
Mahami, Salifu, Hon. 102
Manchester, England 22
Manley, Norman Sir 92, 151
Majority 105, 116, 148, 150
   leader 150
Manu, Agyeman, Hon. 103
Manu, J.W. Hon. 61
Maritime Tribunal 86
Marshal 131
Martial Laws 19
Mason George 74
May, Eskine 11
   Parliamentary Practice 11
Media 97, 107
Parliament and 108
Members of Parliament 36, 42, 52, 60, 68, 71, 98, 108, 109, 112, 113, 114, 117, 121, 129, 131, 140
   election of 56
   First Women of 45-46
   Oath of 62, 68, 84, 104, 105
Memorials of
   Grant, Danquah, Nkrumah - see under individual names
Mensah, E.T. Hon. 73, 81
Mensah Francis Osafo Hon. Dr. 102
Mensah Joseph Henry Hon. 60, 83, 88, 89, 91, 101, 103, 134, 143, 144, 145
Mensah Thomas Dr. 65, 86
Mfantsipim 23
Military Corps 20
Military Officers 20
Military Rule 16
Mills John Evans Atta HE Prof. 81, 84, 86, 100, 134
Milton, John 18,
Mines and factories 75
Ministers of State 31, 38, 65, 68, 70, 71, 83, 88, 90, 96, 112, 113, 114, 116, 119, 122, 123, 131, 144, 145, 146
   advantage of presence in Parliament 123,-124
   appointments of 88, 90, 119, 146, 149, 153
   concerning approval process 146-148
   further legal action 145-146
   parliamentary vetting of 143, 149
   storm over retained stormed budget 144-145
Ministers of State, deputy 83, 88, 90, 144, 145, 146, 148, 152, 153

Ministerial Appointments 153
Ministerial Nominations 90
Ministries 125
Minority 86, 91, 105, 121, 143, 144, 145, 146, 149, 152
   Leader 88, 89, 91, 145, 150, 151
Mitchel, Emma Hon. Mrs. 72
Morkeh, Blay 83
Moslem Association Party 35
Motions of confidence 81
Mukaila Adiba Miss 67
Multiparty Democracy 71, 98, 100, 106, 108, 109, 117, 124
Multiparty Democracy see also Democracy,
   Parliamentary Democracy etc.
Multiparty System of Government 43, 115,
Mumuni, Mohammed, Hon. 81
Munufie, A.A. Hon. 60
Murders 15
Murray, Keith Dr. 25
Nabila, John S. Hon. Dr. 66
Namibia 151
Nandzo, George Hon. 66
Nartey, Richard Dornu Hon. 82, 83
National Alliance of Liberals (NAL) 62
National Assembly 31, 47, 48, 57, 58, 112, 114, 117, 138
   Members of 49
National Assembly see also Parliament
National Commission for Democracy 71
National Convention Party 72, 77, 117
National Democratic Party (NDC) 72, 75, 77, 80, 84, 100, 104, 109, 117, 118, 134, 143
National Economy 105, 107
National Health Scheme 76
National Independent Party 72, 118
National Liberation Council (NLC) 11, 59, 64
National Liberation Movement 27, 29, 35
National Radio 56
National Reconciliation 110
National Reconciliation Act 109
National Reconciliation Commission 107, 110
National Reconciliation Committee 107
National Stadium 87
Nationalism 20
Nduom, Kwesi Hon. Dr. 102
New Patriotic Party (NPP) 72, 84, 100, 104, 109, 118, 134
   Government 109
Newspapers 21

Newspapers see also individual
Newspapers eg. Gold Coast nation
Gold Coast Methodist Times
Gold Coast Chronicle
Gold Coast Echo
Gold Coast Observer etc.
Nigeria 21, 84
Nii Kwabena Bonne III
 (Osu Alata Mache) 25
 anti-inflation Committee 25
Nikoi Amon Hon. Dr. 65
Nimo, Antwi 66
Nixon, Richard 35
Nkansah Lilly Hon. 82
Nketiah Asiedu Hon. 82
Nkrumah Kwame Dr. 11, 16, 20, 22, 23, 25, 26, 33, 34, 40, 41, 42, 43, 44, 45, 48, 46, 50, 54, 56, 58, 59, 69, 96, 97
 concept of African Personality 47, 52
Nkumsah, E.A. 59
Norris John 27
Northern Nigeria
 House of Assembly 37
Northern Peoples Party 35
Northern Region 46
Norwich County Council 39
Nti, Kofi 74
Nunoo, Samuel 66
Nyakotey E.L. Dr. 66
Nyamekye Anna Hon. Mrs. 102
Nyanor Charles Omar Hon. 61, 102
Nyarko Victoria 46
Nylander C.T. Hon. 34
Oath of a Member of Parliament 62, 68, 84, 104, 105
Oath of office 68, 105
Oath of Parliament 46
Obasanjo Olusegun HE of Nigeria 104
Obetsebi-Lamptey E.O 22, 25
Obetsebi Lamptey Jake O. Hon. 101, 135
Obimpeh, Stephen G. Hon. Cdre 72
Ocansey E.N. 53
Ocquaye, Mike Hon. Prof. 122
Ocran A.K. Lt.-Gen. 62
Ocran Kwabena Hon. Dr. 66
Ocran L. T. 67
Official Report see Hansard Official Report.
Ofori-Atta Kofi Asante 34, 46, 56, 57, 59
Ofori-Atta A.E.A. see Ofori-Atta Kofi Asante
Ofori-Atta, Jones Hon. Dr. 61, 70,91
Ofori-Atta, William Hon (Paa Willie) 22, 24, 25, 43, 60
Ohene, Elizabeth Akua Hon. 102

Oil prices 87
Ollenu, Nii Amaa Hon. Justice 61, 62, 120
One Party State 44, 45, 56, 57, 113, 121
Onwona-Agyemang 56
Opoku-Afriyie, Yaw Hon. 66
Opon, S.K. Hon. 61
Opposition 38, 40, 64, 86, 100, 108, 120, 150
 boycott 92
 leader of 38
 parties 27, 77, 118
Order-in-Council 16, 17
Ordinances 16, 17
Ordinances see also Acts
Organisation of African Unity 53
 Conference of Head of States 22, 53
Osafo-Maafo, Yaw Hon 101, 134
Osafo, Mensah Francis Hon. Dr. 102
Osei-Akoto, S. Hon. 61
Osei-Baidoo Hon. 61
Osei-Bonsu, K.G. Hon. 61
Osei M.K. Hon. 61
Osei-Wusu, David Hon. 82
Osei-Wusu, E.M. Hon. Col. 72
Otabil of Gomoa 19
Otoo, Ayikoi 134
Owiredu, Johnathan R. 74
Owusu-Acheampong J.H. Hon. 72, 81, 83
Owusu, Afriyie O. 50, 54
Owusu-Agyemang Hackman Hon. 101, 135
Owusu-Agyepong Felix K. 101, 135
Owusu-Ankomah, Paapa Hon. 103, 134
Owusu-Ansah, Rex Hon. 74, 83, 103, 104
Owusu Comfort Hon. Mrs. 83, 103
Owusu George Hon. 83
Owusu P.K. 74
Owusu Victor Hon. 27, 60
Pan African Congress 22,
Parks and Gardens, Ministry of 53
Parliament 16, 46
 boycotts 25, 151
 British 17
 dissolution of 114
 executive officers 60-62
 First Republic of the,
  of Ghana 36, 57
 independent members of 67, 129
 members of see under members of Parliament
 proceedings on 108
 proclamation summoning 35
 Sitting 93, 143
 State opening of 57, 96, 153
  First Republic 57
  First Parliament 35,-37, 52

167

Second Republic
   First Parliament 62,-64
   Members of Parliament and
      executive officers 60-62
Parliamentarian
   Journal of Parliaments of the
      Commonwealth 80, 91, 153
Parliamentary business 120
Parliamentary Committees see under committees
Parliamentary Democracy 44, 97, 140, 153
Parliamentary elections 72, 121, 118
   (1979) 97
   boycott 118
Parliamentary Elections see also elections
Parliamentary, English 97
Parliamentary Practice 95
   and procedure publication 138
Parliamentary Press 95
   corps 11
Parliamentary Procedure and Practices 116, 138
Parliamentary processes 132
Parliamentary questions see questions
Parliamentary Secretaries 31, 56
Parliamentary Service
   Ghana 12, 95
Parliamentary System 112, 121
Parliamentary Union see Commonwealth Parliamentary Association.
Parties
      central Committee of 54
      minorities 70
      ruling 142
      Representation 35
      Small 129
      Strength 142,
Pe Ayagitan (Chiana Pio) 71
Peace-Keeping 92
   Contribution troops for, in Africa 22
Peasah, Kofi Amankwah 74
Peoples' Convention Party 118
Peoples' Heritage Party 72
Peoples' National Convention 84, 104, 118
Peoples' National Party (PNP) 65, 67, 71, 84, 87, 97, 104, 118
Peoples' Socialist democracy 57
Peprah, Kwame Hon. 81, 91, 144, 146, 147
Peprah Paul K. Hon. 73
Peprah, R. Kwame 72
Pianim E. 62
Plebiscite Act 1960 41
Pogoson, F. Lt. 16
Poku, O.K. Hon. 61

Police Service 58, 64
Political Parties 57, 96, 152
Politics 77, 124, 151
Polling Day 79
Polo ground old 33
Ports and Harbours 75
Positive Change 107
Poverty 106
Powers of approval 149
Prayers 51, 56, 57, 68
Preko, E.I Hon. 55
Prempeh, Kwasi Prof. 122
Prerogative of Mercy 114
President 49, 52, 56, 57, 58, 65, 68, 70, 71, 79, 80, 89, 110, 113, 116, 120, 134, 144, 146, 147, 149, 150, 152, 154-155
   ceremonial (1969) 114
   elect 105
   first 112, 114,
   first see also Nkrumah, Kwame Dr.
   inaugural address 69, 105
   inauguration 84, 85, 149
   scroll of office 69
   swearing-in of 143
President see also Kufour, John Agyekum Nkrumah, Kwame Dr. Akufo-Addo, Edward, Limann, Hilla Dr. etc.
Presidential Commissioin 64
Presidential Elections see Elections Presidential
Presidential System of Government 121, 153
Prevention, Detention Act, 1958 40, 53
Prime Minister 32, 33, 41, 47, 48, 49, 60, 64, 65, 114, 115, 139, 151
   Constitutional instruments 36
"Prison Graduates" 27
Private Members bill 115, 116, 122
Private members questions 70
Private Sector Investment 92
Privileges
   Committee of 126, 128, 129
   of the House 131
   Parliamentary 108
Privy Council 31
Probity, accountability transparency 98
Proclamation 49
Progress Party 60, 62
Progressive Alliance 118
Property-Owning Democracy 107
Provencal, H.S.F. Hon. 55
Provisional National Defence Council (PNDCL) 71, 118
Public Accounts Committee 125, 126, 128, 129, 132, 133

Non-partisan approach to work in 130
Public Holiday 64
Public Galleries 120
Public officials 64, 95, 125
    Dismissal of 568 64
Public service 11
Public Service Commission 42
Pupulampu A.K. 51
Pupulampu A.R. 55
Quakyi, Totobi Hon. 73
Quaidoo, P.K.K. Hon. 34, 50
Quaison-Sackey, Alex Hon. 55, 58
Quarshie, Atto Hon. Dr. 72
Quarshie, R.A. Hon. 60
Quarshigah, Courage Hon. Maj. (rtd) 101, 134
Quashie Ankah Chief of Danadie 15
Quashie Otoo Chief of Abura 15
Quaye Ibrahim Codjoe Hon. Sheikh 83, 102
Quaye, P.O. 56
Queen of Great Britain 15, 30, 31, 36
    Elizabeth R. 36
    message 48
    special representative 31-32
    Victoria 36, 48
Questions 70, 148
Quist, Charles Emmanuel Sir 14, 35, 37, 138
    first speaker 14
    resignation and death of 38
Radio Ghana
    Military in Cooperation with the Police taken over Government of Ghana 59
Rawlings Jerry John HE Flt. Lt. 16, 68, 72, 76, 81, 84, 85, 86, 87, 109, 144
Referendum 45, 72, 77
Regional Assemblies 30, 39, 112
Regional Ministers 83
    Deputy 83
Reindorf Carl D. 61
Reindorf Joe Hon. 66, 124
Representation of the People (Women) bill 45
Republic Day see under Ghana
Resolution 147, 150
Richardson, Oheneba Kwow Hon. 61
Riley-Poku, S.K. Hon. 65
Rio de Janeiro, Brazel 39
Riot Act 25
Roads 75
Robberies 15
Royal Charter 17
Royal instructions 17

Rule of Law 106
Rules and Regulations 16
Saaka, Yakubu Dr. 66
Sackey J.H. 35, 51
Saddique, Boniface Abubakar Hon. 102, 135
Safo-Adu Kwame Hon. Dr. 60
Sagoe, J.E 35
Sahanum, Mogtari Hon. 102
Sahibs Pukka 40
Saint Augustine, 20
Saint Augustine's College 27
Saint Paul 24
Sakyi-Hughes, Ebenezer Begyina Hon. 134
Salaries and Wages 65
Salia, Edward Hon. 73, 81
Salifu, Abdullah Hon. 82
Salifu, Ben Hon. 102
Sallah Edward 64
Saltpond 22
Samson Argonistes 18
Sanitation National Policy 87
Sarbah, John 17
Sawyerr, H.R. Hon. 66, 72
Scheck, Saki Hon. 61
Second World War 37-38
    Soldiers 24
Secondary Schools 23
Secondary Schools see also Saint Augustine, Adisadel, Ghana National College etc.
Secret ballot 39
Security of State 25, 53
Seidu, Amadu, Hon. Alh. 73, 83
Seidu, M.A. Hon. Alhaji 83
Sekan, Nii Adjei-Boye Hon. 83
Select Committee 133, 126
Self-Government 22, 23, 24
Self-Rule 18, 19
Selormey, Victor 73, 82
Senkyire, Baffour Kwabena 55
Separation of Powers 116
Sessional Address 52, 57, 62, 75, 77, 86, 113, 119, 147
Sienti, Nana 135
Sierra Leone 20, 21
Slavery 20
Smith, Ian 59
Sofo, Seidu Alex Hon. 103
Social Democratic Front 67
Social Security Act 1965 53
South Africa 86
South African Workshop 151
Southern Rhodesia Independence 59

Sowu, C.M.K. Sqn Ldr (rted) 72
Speaker 31, 35, 37,-38, 46, 48, 49, 51, 52,
    53, 71, 84, 85, 88, 93, 94, 95, 96, 97, 98,
    118, 129, 130, 131, 140, 1432, 145, 146,
    147, 148, 155,-157
    attendance of 700th anniversary celebration in London 57
    chair 32, 57, 41
    deputy 39, 96, 104, 118
    oath 39, 51, 56, 62, 75, 84, 104
Spectator, Daily 21
Speech 108
    Of acceptance 51, 62, 68, 75, 84, 104
    Interrupting 95
Spio-Garbrah, Ekwow Hon. 81
Sports 87
Standing Committee 128, 129
    Comparison with House of Commons 128
Standing Orders 89, 119, 127, 129, 138, 146, 150
Standing Orders Committee 126, 127, 128, 129
Stapley
    London Tutor Goldsmith 47
Star of West Africa 21
State drums 52
State House Complex Conference Hall 62
State of Emergency 25
State of the nation
    first message to Parliament Feb 15 2001, 106
State opening of Parliament see Parliament
    State Opening of
State Planning Commission 58
Statutory Corporation Act 53
Stevenson, R.L. 18
Sub-judice Convention 121
Subsidiary Legislation Committee 128
"Suffering masses" 24
Sulemana, Amidu Hon. Alhaji 73, 82
Superior Court of Judicature 65
Supreme Court 64, 71, 89, 90, 140, 142, 144, 145, 146, 147-148, 152
Swanzy F. & A 21
Tachie, K.E.K. 62, 74, 103
Tachie Kenneth Kofi 83
Tachie-Menson F.E. Hon. 55
Tagoe, Paul 56
Tagoe Theresa Hon. Ms 103
Tagoe Wulff 66
Tali, Yakubu (Tolon-Na) 39, 51, 56
Tarrant, William 24

Taxes 77, 122
Tetteh Emmanuel Maj. (rtd) 73
Third Republic see Ghana Third Republic
Thomas, Wynford Vaughan 35
Thompson K.O. 51, 55
Tia Johnson Hon. 103
Togoland Congress Party 35
Togoland Southern 18
Tolon-Na see Tali, Yakubu (Tolon-Na)
Torto, E.T. Hon. 66
Tosu, Leonard Peace 51, 67, 68
Toure, Ahmed Sekou 58, 69
Tourism 76
Trades Union Congress (TUC) 26, 44
Transitional Constitution of 1954 112
Transitional Provisions of order in Council 31
Treason 42
Twumasi, E.K. 67
UGCC
    Inauguration of the 23, 24
Unilateral Declaration of independence
    Southern Rhodesia 29
Union Government of Africa 22, 53
Union of Socialist Soviet Republic (USSR) 37
United Action Party 62
United Africa Company 21
United Gold Coast Convention 9, 22
United Kingdom 30, 59
    Trusteeship 18
United National Convention 67
United Nationalist Party 62
United Nations Organisation 39, 71,
    Secretary General 78, 86, 92
    Secretary-General see also Annan, Kofi
United Party 51
United States of America
Universal Adult Suffrage 112
    Presidents powers 117
Urban Development 87
Ussher Fort Prison 26
Value Added Tax 91
Value Added Tax (VAT) Act of 1995 77
Van Dyck Dr. 66
Vanderpuije, John Chief 17
Vaughan Williams Peter 73
Vetting see Ministers of State
Victoria Queen of England (1837-1901) 16
Volta Region 46
    Parliamentary Vetting
Vox Populi 21
Wade, Abdoulaye, H.E. 104

Walkout
   Minority 109
Waters, John see also Ayensu Kobina
Watson Aiken 25
Watson Report 26
Welbeck N.A Hon. 34, 54
Welsing, John 59
West African Herald 21
West African Settlements 18
Western Echo 21
Western Region 46
Westminster
   System of Government 94, 119, 121, 123, 138
Whips 123
   US Congress 125
Whole House
   Committee of the 130
Wilmot Christiana Hon. 46
Witnesses 131, 132
Wolfenson, James D. 91, 92
Women members of Parliament 45, 46, 78, 134
Women members of Parliament see also under individual women MPs. Eg.
   Tagoe, Theresa
World Bank 91
Wussah, J.N. 67
Yakubu, Hawa Hon. Mrs. 102
Yanka, Kojo Hon. 82
Yeboah-Afari B. 34
Yaboah, Kwesi Owusu 102
Yeboah S.Y 50, 55
Yeboah Vida A. Hon. Mrs. 72, 81
Yirenkyi, Janet Mrs. 66
Zanlerigu, David Hon. Col 66
Zero Tolerance 106
Ziedong, Bede 74
Zimbabwe 29
Zuma Jacob H.E 105